Surround Sound

Surround Sound

Rev. Birdella A. Tucker and Rev. Mary Renteria

To order additional copies of this book, contact:
Xlibris Corporation
1-888-795-4274
www.Xlibris.com
Orders@Xlibris.com
38519

Contents

Introduction

"Praise Him with the sounding of the trumpet" (Psalm 150:3). Prayer is a sound that comes from us to surround the throne of God either in worship of Him, petitions to Him, or the sound of God's judgments. There are prayers from our souls and then there are prayers containing the sound of "spiritual authority."

Spiritual authority prayers are those empowered by His Spirit when the soul of man submits to His voice. The focus of this book centers on the prayers submitted to the "sounds" of God in the past, present, and future.

"Then the man and his wife heard the sound of the Lord God as he was walking in the garden in the cool of the day" (Genesis 3:8). Past.

"Suddenly a sound like the blowing of a violent wind came from heaven and filled the whole house where they were sitting" (Acts 2:2).Present.

"The fifth angel sounded his trumpet, and I saw a star that had fallen from the sky to the earth" (Revelation 9:1). Future.

Chapter 1

The Sound Of Learning

God's voice is wooing us to learn from Him different sounds of prayers. Throughout the ages there has been a "sound" that has been heard by those who would listen. We have heard the sound of repentance, the sound of healing, the sound of the Word of God, the sound of war, the sound of warnings and the sound of redemption, to name a few. There will be two new sounds for today, the sound of the prodigal's return and the sound of compensation. For each type of prayer there is a certain sound of which the intercessor needs to be aware.

In Isaiah 28:23-29 God tells us that just as there are different types of crops and different methods in which to harvest these crops, God has different methods in which to teach us.

23. Listen and hear my voice; pay attention and hear what I say.
24. When a farmer plows for planting, does he plow continually? Does he keep on breaking up and harrowing the soil?
25. When he has leveled the surface, does he not sow caraway and scatter cumin? Does he not plant wheat in its place, barley in its plot, and spelt in its field?
26. His God instructs him and teaches him the right way.
27. Caraway is not threshed with a sledge, nor is a cartwheel rolled over cumin; caraway is beaten out with a rod, and cumin with a stick.
28. Grain must be ground to make bread; so one does not go on threshing it forever. Though he drives the wheels of his threshing cart over it, his horses do not grind it.
29. All this also comes from the Lord Almighty, wonderful in counsel and magnificent in wisdom.

Just as the Old Testament was a schoolmaster to instruct us in certain sounds, there are sounds today that the Holy Spirit wants us to hear. These sounds will join the past and the present to change the future. These sounds will reveal our mistakes as well as instruct us in harvesting the seeds of the past. God is calling us to prayer—God is looking for those who will pray—God will teach us how to pray. The question is, will we pray? Will we ask the Creator of prayer to open our ears to hear Him?

Jeremiah 33:2-3 says, "This is what the Lord says, he who made the earth, the Lord who formed it and established it—the Lord is his name: Call to me and I will answer you and tell you great and unsearchable things you do not know."

God requires that we ask Him for the things that we need, whether they be answers to a given situation or material needs. He doesn't get mad when we seek His face for answers. The questions that we ask are merely a vehicle in which to correspond with Him. They allow us an opportunity to communicate with our Creator to learn His heart.

God desires to take up an abode with us and to walk and talk with us as He did with Adam in the Garden of Eden. Can we hear this sound? It will take seeing and hearing from Him how we have departed from His presence. And, in the case of intercession, we have to hear what God has for others. For most of us, the voice of God has been stolen because of sin. But, in Isaiah 6 we read that Isaiah heard the sound of voices crying "Holy, holy, holy is the Lord Almighty." He then heard the sounds of conviction coming from his heart as the iniquities within were revealed. Our ears became dull from hearing because of sin. This being the case, when sin is addressed the ears can become open to the sound of holiness once again. We can walk and talk with God in His kingdom on earth by manifesting His presence.

To manifest the kingdom of God, we need to know what the kingdom is and what God expects of us. When Jesus came to earth, He told the people that the kingdom of heaven is at hand, and that we are to make ready the way of the Lord, and to make His paths straight. Jesus went about all Galilee teaching in their synagogues, proclaiming the gospel of the kingdom, and healing every kind of disease and sickness among the people. While He was with His disciples, He taught them kingdom principles and revealed the Father to them. Kingdom means royalty, rule, and realm. In this kingdom there will be established authority to rule.

Sovereignty

A kingdom's foundation is on the principle of sovereignty. God is sovereign in His kingdom in heaven and will be on earth. He has chosen us to manifest His kingdom as joint heirs with His Son, Jesus Christ, who is the Word incarnate. The Holy Spirit gives power to those entrusted with these kingdom principles. Power means force, ability, strength, might, substance, and wealth. This power comes by only one way, through the blood covenant which is established at the time of our rebirth.

Most assuredly, I say to you, unless one is born of water and the Spirit, he cannot enter the kingdom of God, (John 3:5).

Jesus is the door to the kingdom. He who does not enter through the door is a thief and a robber. But he who enters by the door is the shepherd of the sheep. Jesus is the door of the sheep. He who enters by Him shall be saved (John 10:1-2).

The channel between God's kingdom in heaven and His kingdom on earth is Jesus Christ. He is the door that we go through to the Father. Those who pass through this door are called "saved." Yeshua, Jesus' given name in Hebrew, means salvation. Salvation is the acknowledging of one's inability to receive from God on one's own merits. The voice of self has been quieted, (temporarily), so that the sound of God's Spirit can be heard.

Our pilgrimage begins the moment that we believe in Jesus and receive Him as our Savior. A pilgrimage, according to The American College Dictionary, means a journey, (especially a long one) made to some sacred place. On this journey we learn truths about the kingdom of God so that we can establish them on earth as they affect our prayer life. Let us begin with the Lord's Prayer found in Matthew 6.

9. Our Father in heaven, hallowed be your name,
10. Your kingdom come, your will be done on earth as it is in heaven,
11. Give us today our daily bread.
12. Forgive us our debts, as we also have forgiven our debtors,
13. And lead us not into temptation, but deliver us from the evil one.

Hallowed be His name

The first truth is this; God's name is hallowed and we are to respond to Him and to His name with respect and reverence. I cannot expect to have power with God and not be in submission to Him. He will not give His authority to anyone who does not honor Him and see Him as holy.

The second truth we are to learn is that it is God's will for His kingdom to be established on earth through us. To do this, we have to hear His voice daily. If we do not know that it is God's ultimate will to establish His authority on earth, then how can we pray with authority if we do not submit to the established authority in the land?

Jesus then prays for us to forgive others as we want to be forgiven. There is always a voice of repentance sounding when we commit sin. When we do not listen to this voice, then our hearts become hardened to the point that we will not hear the Holy Spirit when He speaks to us.

Hardness of heart also happens when we do not forgive those who have trespassed against us. In our hurt we can turn a deaf ear to God (Acts 28:26-27).

The next part of the prayer, "Lead us not into temptation," suggests that the Holy Spirit will speak to us to avoid certain things. If we can only hear His voice more clearly, we would avoid many a disaster. Remember, God wants us to pray to hear the leading of His Spirit.

Prayers that contain "spiritual authority" hinges on obedience to the voice of God

It is obedience to the Word that opens our eyes and ears to the voice of the Holy Spirit who teaches us the rules of the kingdom. Each time we obey His rules, our prayer life becomes more effectual to the pulling down of strongholds. Obedience is the sacrifice that we offer to Him.

In the Old Testament, when a sacrifice was placed on the altar and accepted by God, it was consumed. Smoke rose toward heaven as this evidence. Prayer is the sacrifice that we lay on the altar, (Jesus). The evidence that God accepts this sacrifice will be seen in the building of His kingdom. We need to be as Nehemiah who said, "The God of heaven will give us success; therefore we, His servants, will arise and build."

Prayer is building God's kingdom on earth as it is in heaven

The blueprint for our earthly habitation is in heaven. Prayer releases this information but we still have to do the work released. We have to ask for His plans as seen in the following scriptures:

Thou wilt show me the path of life: in thy presence is fullness of joy; at thy right hand are pleasures for evermore (Psalm 16:11).

That I may know Him, and the power of his resurrection, and the fellowship of his sufferings, made conformable unto his death (Philippians 3:10).

Jesus became man for us to conform to His divinity. Prayer aids in the transformation by speaking His Word to create the identity that is lacking. Praying His Word produces the image needed for the change. Prayer answering the command to look to Jesus and not at the circumstance as seen in the following:

Look to Me, and be saved, all you ends of the earth! For I am God, and there is no other (Isaiah 45:22).

For God did not send His Son into the world to condemn the world, but that the world through Him might be saved (John 3:17).

For God so loved the world that He gave His only begotten Son that whoever believes in Him should not perish but have everlasting life (John 3:16).

Prayer is the manifestation of God's love

The act of praying reveals God's love in the intercessor and the act of love to those being prayed for. Prayer is like a contract that binds those being prayed for to the cross where Jesus interprets our prayers. Prayer is God's love in action. I have to receive His love into my heart before I can love Him back with true, effectual prayer.

Man was born in sin. Without the ability to love as God, our prayers are self-induced. True love, the agape love, only comes through identification with Jesus. It is written in the Bible that everything will produce after like kind. If I love God with all of my heart and pray in this love, then there will be evidence, fruit of these prayers.

Paul says that we are to pray that Christ may dwell in our hearts through faith, being rooted and grounded in love, so that we can comprehend Him, (Ephesians 3:17). If I do not bring Him glory and honor through my prayers, then my love for Him can be questioned. Philippians 2:1-2 says:

1.   If you have any encouragement from being united with Christ, if any comfort from his love, if any fellowship with the Spirit, if any tenderness and compassion,

2. then make my joy complete by being like-minded, having the same love, being one in spirit and purpose.

Obedience to the Word is an act of love which brings results

II John 6 says, "And this is love: that we walk in obedience to his commands. As you have heard form the beginning, his command is that you walk in love."

We can revise this last scripture verse with the word "pray" according to His commandments. As we continue to read, we will learn that there are prayers which are not after either His commandments or His love; therefore these prayers will not be after the mind of Christ.

Love continues in the teaching of Christ.

Prayer is submitting to God's teaching and is to be continued all the days of our lives, not just once in awhile when we get into a tough spot. We didn't receive the gift of love only once. Prayer is love in action. He who dwells in this love dwells and continues in Him. Jesus' walk upon the earth was a walk of love and forgiveness. If we love (pray), we will forgive those who have sinned against us. Failure to forgive reveals a failure to love as Christ and will stop the flow of our prayers to God.

It is the love of God in man that calls
for the things of the Spirit

It is His love that is willing to give himself for others. The scriptures also define God's being as Light. Light means illumination, to make clear, to understand, to ascend, grow, prefer, rise, increase, and cause to ascend. The following scripture shows that those who do not walk in the light will not have the image which reflects the light.

2. For we have renounced the hidden things of shame, not walking in craftiness nor handling the word of God deceitfully, but by manifestation of the truth commending ourselves to every man's conscience in the sight of God.

3. But even if our gospel is veiled, it is veiled to those who are perishing,

4. whose minds the god of this age has blinded, who do not believe, lest the light of the gospel of the glory of Christ, who is the image of God, should shine on them (II Corinthians 4:2-4).

5. And this is the condemnation, that light is come into the world, and men loved darkness rather than light, because their deeds were evil (John 3:19).

Prayer releases light to shine on those who are in darkness so that they can see the way they are to go

In Revelation 9:18, it says that one-third of the world will be killed by the three plagues . . . Yet the people repented not of their sins. If our eyes are on death (sin), then we will see death. The truth is hidden from us until we turn to the "Light." I John 1:1-4 reveals this truth:

1. That which was from the beginning, which we have heard, which we have seen with our eyes, which we have looked at and our hands have touched—this we proclaim concerning the Word of life.

2. The life appeared; we have seen it and testify to it, and we proclaim to you the eternal life, which was with the Father and has appeared to us.

3. We proclaim to you what we have seen and heard, so that you also may have fellowship with us. And our fellowship is with the Father and with his Son, Jesus Christ.

4. We write this to make our joy complete.

This is what prayer does; it brings forth the word of truth and comfort to those who are in darkness so that they will not fall away from God.

Negativism hinders the light of God's Word to us

When a person focuses on the negative situations in which he finds himself, then God has to raise someone up to pray the light of God's Word for him. When the light is seen, all rejoice. The Word says, "Look up!" Turn to the light and see your salvation.

Without the light to reveal the Word, we will walk in the craftiness of our minds and ask questions that are kept in darkness and lose fellowship with the Father

Questions that keep us in darkness might sound like this: "Does God love me?" "Does God even care what happens to me?" These questions are contradictions to the Word of God. For the first question, it is written is Romans 5:8, "But God demonstrated his own love for us in this: While we were still sinners, Christ died for us." And for the second question, "Cast all your anxiety on him because he cares for you," (I Peter 5:7).

A person walking in darkness refracts the light (the Word of the Lord) and will often attempt to convince others that God cannot be trusted and that we cannot believe in His Word. Only the true light will reveal the Father and the Son. The Spirit will expose any other light to those who have come into fellowship with the Father. "For with you is the foundation of life; In your light we see light," (Psalm 36:9).

If what people are telling us does not bring forth the good news of the gospel, which is life, then it is not the light we should follow. The light comes to expose areas in our lives which need to be corrected. Man has been born in iniquity and sin, but until the Word comes to reveal and stir up these areas, we cannot change.

The reason the light comes to reveal areas of impurity is God's love perfecting us into the image of His Son. Let us therefore walk in the light as He is in the light.

The light will consume the flesh if we yield our flesh to it

Satan knows the Word and how to use it against us. Isn't it time for us to know and use the Word to deliver others? Prayers are like a flame of fire that consumes evil. It says in Hebrews 1:7, "And of the angels He says, Who makes His angels winds, and His ministers a flame of fire." This fire that the Lord is speaking of refers to those who are obedient to Him.

We are his ministers on earth, but will one day be above the angels because we will be at the right hand of God in Christ Jesus. If we are to be as ministers of fire for God, then we have to know the God of fire. Fire is God's nature. Nature means the power that regulates the world.

There are four types of fire that reveal the nature of God which we are to represent:

1. **In the burning bush. (Exodus 3)**

Moses turned aside to see this strange phenomenon. When God is about to send us out in prayer, He reveals His plan to us, yet we are not consumed by His presence.

2. **As tongues of fire. (Acts 2)**

When we speak His Words, the plans of the enemy are destroyed.

3. **Baptism by fire by the spirit of judgment. (Isaiah 4)**

The words that we speak clarify sin.

4. **Consuming fire on all unbelievers.**
   (Isaiah 9 & Jeremiah 5:14)

If we learn that the fire of God speaks, then we will see lives changed when we speak under His authority. People will turn aside to ask of the power in us.

We cannot fellowship with the Lord outside of the blood

Fellowshipping in the Blood of Christ speaks for us. "In that day a fountain will be opened for the house of David and for the inhabitants of Jerusalem for sin and for uncleanness," (Zechariah 13:1).

The fountain that this is speaking of is the blood and the water which flowed from Jesus. Notice, the blood and the water are fountains of life, a wellspring flowing continually. The blood was for the cleansing of our sins; the water was for the cleansing of our iniquities with the Word. The blood covenant was the means by which we obtained oneness with God. By obedience to this covenant we would receive health, wealth, power, and established authority. It says in Deuteronomy 8,

> 1. Be careful to follow every command I am giving you today, so that you may live and increase and may enter and possess the land that the Lord promised on oath to your forefathers.

In order to expect the promises of the covenant, we need to know what a covenant is. Strong's definition and its references from #1285 first. A covenant is the sense of cutting, a compact by passing between pieces of flesh, a confederacy, or league. The next reference says, #1262 which means to feed, to render clearly, to choose, to cause to eat, to manifest, and to give meat.

When we are in covenant with someone, we can expect that person to give us help in time of need, whether it is food, provision, finances, or protection; and they are to expect us to fulfill our end of the compact.

The covenant we have with the Father is through His Son, Jesus

Jesus gave His flesh to be cut for us. In the cutting, provision was made for us to enter His kingdom and receive His protection and resources. Our covenant gives us permission to ask our Father for our needs. If we are not in covenant with God (a Christian living as a non-believer), then our asking Him for things draw satanic influences resulting in (demonization) or demonic affliction to the Christian. James 4:1-8 helps us see that a Christian who holds bitterness, jealousy, unforgiveness, etc., allows access into his flesh, mind, and spirit.

1. What causes fights and quarrels among you? Don't they come from your desires that battle within you?

2. You want something but don't get it. You kill and covet, but you cannot have what you want. You quarrel and fight. You do not have, because you do not ask God.

3. When you ask, you do not receive, because you ask with wrong motives, that you may spend what you get on your pleasures.

4. You adulterous people, don't you know that friendship with the world is hatred toward God? Anyone who chooses to be a friend of the world becomes an enemy of God.

5. Or do you think Scripture says without reason that the spirit he caused to live in us envies intensely?

6. But he gives us more grace. That is why Scripture says: "God opposes the proud but gives grace to the humble.

7. Submit yourselves, then, to God. Resist the devil, and he will flee from you.

8. Come near to God and he will come near to you. Wash your hands, you sinners, and purify your hearts, you double-minded."

Demonization is demonic attachment

Dr. Ed Murphy, from his book on The Handbook for Spiritual Warfare (page 510) says demonization is demonic attachment that has come because the believer has not denounced the satanic influences which have entered. He says,

> The two-fold fruit of these bitter, prideful, negative emotions is revealed in James 3:16. First, there is "disorder." God's order is violated. There is confusion and lack of peace within, tension, broken relationships, and hurt feelings with others. Second is what James calls "every evil thing." These prideful, negative attitudes are the open door to all kinds of potential evil (Hebrews 12:15). Sin energy, like a mighty negative spiritual magnet, draws Satan and his demons. Where deep interpersonal conflicts exist among believers, the Evil One is there. Such conflict with others cannot be accepted in our homes, churches, or even in our communities. Better to suffer harm ourselves than to harm others, especially those who are part of the body of Christ.

God is presenting His church (the bride of Christ) without spot or wrinkle. Those who are His will be purified and made white. These are they that have overcome the devil by the blood of the Lamb, the word of their testimony, and the fact that they did not love their life even to death. Just recently I had more revelation or understanding on this last stipulation, "Did not love their life even to the death." It is speaking of a people who are identifying with Christ in His death, burial, and resurrection power. These are the ones who overcome Satan because there is nothing in them that belongs to him (Revelation 12:11).

Transformation is the objective of prayer

God's objective for those who live in His kingdom is that they're transformed into His image. The water that poured forth from the side of Jesus was living water. Just as the Father is the fountain of living water spoken of in Jeremiah 2:13, Jesus declares Himself to be this living water in John 4:10. "But whoever drinks of the water that I shall give him will never thirst. But the water that I give will become in him a fountain of water springing up into everlasting life" (John 4:14). Prayer is drinking from living water.

An unthankful person will not pray

It says in the book of Romans that because of a spirit of unthankfulness, we are taken away from God in our minds and become unfruitful. If we are unthankful to God, then how are we going to come to Him and ask from Him? We won't. It is through knowing Jesus that we are able to come to the Father and ask things of Him. If we refuse to learn of Jesus, our hearts become darkened and we begin to do such things which are not becoming to the plan of God. Is there hope for such? Yes, our hope is in the blood of Jesus for the remission of sin (Romans 5:5). His blood is the only blood which washes and renews our minds from sin (I John 1:9).

Prayers are defiled by bitterness

God admonishes us in Hebrews 12 to look diligently into our hearts and minds to see if there is anything which does not line up with the Word of God. Any root of bitterness from the enemy can spring up and cause trouble, and thereby many are defiled. God has given us a responsibility to present ourselves to Him—to cleanse ourselves, and to give ourselves to the working of the Holy Spirit who will mortify all deeds of the flesh. Those who are thirsty for the things of God can come freely and obtain this life-giving water. The Word is perpetual, flowing without end; and the blood is a continual fountain.

We must apply this fountain of blood and water to ourselves spirit, soul, and body. Satan drops thoughts into our minds and then, if they are not driven out, a stronghold is placed in our hearts causing us to speak out that which was thought upon. If we do not renew our hearts and minds with the Word, we will be led astray. Many people believe that they do not need to receive the blood for the renewing of their minds. This is not so. It is written in I John 1:7-9:

7. But if we walk in the light, as he is in the light, we have fellowship with one another, and the blood of Jesus, his Son, purifies us from all sin.
8. If we claim to be without sin, we deceive ourselves and the truth is not in us.
9. If we confess our sins, he is faithful and just and will forgive us our sins and purify us from all unrighteousness.

Dead works must be identified to keep prayer alive

We need to identify dead works in order to apply the blood for cleansing. Anything which causes our minds to think on things which are not under the control of the Holy Spirit needs cleansing. Feeding our minds on the system of darkness, fantasies, vain philosophy, soap operas, etc., are all areas which need to be confessed as sin.

If we think we can walk a Christian life and hold on to things in the mind which are not proper, then try to approach the throne of God, we deceive ourselves into thinking that we can manifest the presence of God and get answers from Him. This is like the sin of Achan who hid a Babylonian garment in the floor of his tent (Joshua 7). It is a type of our hiding things in our minds thinking God doesn't see our thoughts. Turn to Ezekiel 8:

6. Son of man, do you see what they are doing—the utterly detestable things the house of Israel is doing here, things that will drive me far from my sanctuary? But you will see things that are even more detestable.'

7. Then he brought me to the entrance to the court. I looked, and I saw a hole in the wall.

8. He said to me, 'Son of man, now dig into the wall.' So I dug into the wall and saw a doorway there.

9. And he said to me, 'Go in and see the wicked and detestable things they are doing here.'

10. So I went in and looked, and I saw portrayed all over the walls all kinds of crawling things and detestable animals and all the idols of the house of Israel.

God sees our thoughts when we pray

We cannot hide evil thoughts from God and think that He does not know. Iniquities and sin begin in the mind first. Satan wants to introduce thoughts of doubt about our Father—that He is uncaring and will not answer our prayers. Those who believe this lie will cease to come to Him and ask anything from Him. Next, after Satan has the mind, he will reach out to possess the heart of man, and then take the whole man into captivity. Before Eve sinned, she considered in her mind and reasoned in her heart that what Satan told her was good. (Genesis 3:6-24). When they felt separated from

God, they ceased to come to Him. God had to make the first step and ask Adam, "Where are you?"

Just as Adam and Eve couldn't hide from God neither can we hide evil thoughts from Him. All evil thoughts have to be revealed and brought to the blood of Christ before we can follow on with God in the spirit of truth.

We are to follow God by the Spirit, not by what our minds think to be true. When the children of Israel stepped into the Red Sea, which was a type of their deliverance, they had to do it by faith. If they had looked at the natural circumstance and considered reasons why they should not step into the water, they would not have been protected from their enemies. God places us at "Red Sea" situations all of the time. Whenever we step into prayer and ignore our flesh, we will grow in the spirit of truth. We will then become stronger in prayer. We have an example of this in John 5:1-7:

2.   Now there is in Jerusalem near the Sheep Gate a pool, which in Aramaic is called Bethesda and which is surrounded by five covered colonnades.

3, 4.   Here a great number of disabled people used to lie—the blind, the lame, the paralyzed.

5.   One who was there had been an invalid for thirty-eight years.

6.   When Jesus saw him lying there and learned that he had been in this condition for a long time, he asked him, 'Do you want to get well?'

7.   'Sir,' the invalid replied, 'I have no one to help me into the pool when the water is stirred. While I am trying to get in, someone else goes down ahead of me.'

We can see clearly how this man almost missed his healing. His thoughts on his condition spoke a voice that almost rejected the voice of God. In the same way, if we listen to our fears and circumstances we can **not** hear the prayer God has sent to us to "take up our bed and walk."

Had the man stayed in the things he could see or feel, he would have stayed sick. But he acted on the Word and received his healing, which was a manifestation of God's presence. The Word is life. The five senses must be put under subjection to the Word. I believe by the Spirit of the Lord, that when we face situations in life where the waters which surround us seem troubled, if we would hear God's Word we would be healed.

Prayer positions our self to represent God

Prayer is a type of positioning ourselves to represent God and man. It is a sacrifice that affects the total of man and is therefore a seed to receive from God when we have a need spirit, soul, or body. Prayer is coming to God to be built into a spiritual house as seen in I Peter 2:4-5:

4. As you come to him, the living Stone—rejected by men but chosen by God and precious to him,
5. you also like living stones, are being built into a spiritual house to be a holy priesthood, offering spiritual sacrifices acceptable to God through Jesus Christ.

Jesus, our High Priest, sanctified Himself first so that we can be sanctified and perform the duties as His priests on earth by our prayers. Turn to John 17:14-19:

14. I have given them your word and the world has hated them for they are not of the world any more than I am of the world.
15. My prayer is not that you take them out of the world but that you protect them from the evil one.
16. they are not of the world, even as I am not of it.
17. Sanctify them by the truth; your word is truth.
18. As you sent me into the world, I have sent them into the world.
19. For them I sanctify myself, that they too may be truly sanctified.

Those who pray must sanctify themselves

Sanctify means to purify, make clean, and be separate. We are worthy to come to Him in prayer because we have been sanctified for this work by Jesus, Himself. Those who are sanctified in Jesus are of His seed; and God said to those who are of this seed, "Surely blessing I will bless thee." (Hebrews 6:14). God blesses us when we pray for others.

Jesus came to converse with man. He came as the express image of the Father to convey His thoughts to us. He has placed within man, through His Son, the ability to reason and communicate. Without this, man could not hear from God. Thus, he would not seek after God to be like Him. Knowing God comes through the "rebirth." It is being born not of corruptible seed but eternal seed from the heavenly Father.

Prayer is applying God's Word to a situation

God has given us the Word and has told us how to use the Word. It is our responsibility to apply it to our lives. Failure to do so causes a breach in our covenant with the blood. God does not break the covenant. Any failure to walk in all that is written in the covenant is due to a failure on our part. If we lack wisdom in any area, we are to ask the Holy Spirit to reveal this area to us and to give us understanding. God is not looking for loopholes to hurt us. He has sent us His Spirit to teach us and to bring us into all truth. The Word is two-fold:

1. It reveals the character and nature of God.
2. It reveals the sins and iniquities within man.

Prayer is a seed planted in Christ

It is written in Mark 4 that the Word is like a seed that is planted in our hearts. When persecution arises, the Word will reveal the condition of the soil in which the Word was planted. Are there thorns? Rocks? If the Word has a good place to grow, fruit will be produced.

The enemy comes to take away the Word. It is our responsibility to prepare our hearts to receive the Word. Proverbs 16:1 says, "To man belong the plans of the heart, but from the Lord comes the reply of the tongue." And, in Romans 10:9-10, "That if you confess with your mouth, 'Jesus is Lord,' and believe in your heart that God raised him from the dead, you will be saved. For it is with your heart that you believe and are justified."

It is our responsibility to purify our hearts. James 4:8 says, "Come near to God and he will come near to you. Wash your hands, you sinners, and purify your hearts, you double-minded." I Peter 3:15 says, "But in your hearts set apart Christ as Lord. Always be prepared to give the reason for the hope that you have. But do this with gentleness and respect."

Unless the heart is prepared to serve, God we will not be able to deliver that Word in the power God expects. The reason is found in James 1:20. "For man's anger does not bring about the righteous life that God desires." If we refuse to prepare our hearts before we stand up to deliver God's Word, then a door is opened for the enemy to come and attack us. Part of the preparation of the heart involves listening to the sound of the Holy Spirit who will reveal the iniquities within.

Groaning of uneasiness in our spirit is prayer

There are times that we hear the sound of "uneasiness" within. Without addressing this we become like the statement, "Fools rush in where angels fear to tread." An uneasy feeling is just one way in which we can be taught how to follow the Lord. If we allow uneasiness to remain inside without addressing it, we can be taken on a detour from the object of our mission. Often uneasiness is a signal that we are to judge our thoughts of fear. At other times uneasiness is the flesh's way of telling us that it does not want to do what the Lord has asked of us.

I'm sure Jonah was uneasy when he received the word to go to Nineveh. His failure to bring this feeling to God resulted in his disobedience in going another direction from the one God intended for him. We do the same. There are times that a word comes to us from a prophetic utterance, but the person giving the word is questionable. Without establishing first whether the word is from God or not we will not be able to give ourselves to the word. God tells us that we become established in the word given to us by the prophets if we believe the prophets (II Chronicles 20:20). Belief is crucial to obedience.

The prophets are used as God's messengers to the people in like manner as the priests. As the priest goes to the Father on behalf of others to repent and to seek God's face for them in prayer, a prophet hears God's Words and speaks them verbally.

When we receive a word from God that we do not understand, we can go to our Father and ask Him to clarify His instructions. We are told in Romans 8:26, "The Spirit helps us in our weakness. We do not know what we ought to pray for, but the Spirit himself intercedes for us with groans that words cannot express."

We can actually feel the groaning of the Holy Spirit when He intercedes for us. When His work is complete, clarity comes to us and we enter into a rest. This type of prayer is warring against a stronghold in the mind. II Corinthians 10:3-6 are such scriptures.

3.   For though we live in the world, we do not wage war as the world does.

4. The weapons we fight with are not the weapons of the world. On the contrary, they have divine power to demolish strongholds.

5. We demolish arguments and every pretension that sets itself up against the knowledge of God, and we take captive every thought to make it obedient to Christ.

6. And we will be ready to punish every act of disobedience, once your obedience is complete.

These strongholds are placed there in our minds and emotions by the devil himself. There is only one way to pull them down and that is by the weapons given to us by the Holy Spirit. Ephesians 6 gives us a list of our armor in which to accomplish this:

10. Finally, be strong in the Lord and in His mighty power.

11. Put on the full armor of God so that you can take your stand against the devil's schemes.

12. For our struggle is not against flesh and blood, but against the rulers, against the authorities, against the powers of this dark world and against the spiritual forces of evil in the heavenly realms.

13. Therefore put on the full armor of god, so that when the day of evil comes, you may be able to stand your ground, and after you have done everything, to stand.

14. Stand firm then, with the belt of truth buckled around your waist, with the breastplate of righteousness I place,

15. And with your feet fitted with the readiness that comes form the gospel of peace.

16. In addition to all this, take up the shield of faith, with which you can extinguish all the flaming arrows of the evil one.

17. Take the helmet of salvation and the sword of the Spirit, which is the word of God.

18. And pray in the Spirit on all occasions with all kinds of prayers and requests. With this in mind, be alert and always keep on praying for all the saints.

It takes total obedience to the Word of God to pull down the devil's powers. Satan knows that if we have doubts and questions in our minds regarding God's faithfulness, we will be defeated.

Prayer is standing alongside of Jesus

When we realize that God wants us to be alongside of Him in our prayers, we will be more at ease in our approach to Him. Our goal should be to become mature in Him, to become all that Jesus Christ is, and to approach the throne boldly without fear. This is done by the Holy Spirit. He exposes self-will, resentfulness, stubbornness, etc., which are the iniquities of the soul nature. Power to be bold is called "exousia" which means ability, privilege, force, capacity, liberty, and strength in the Greek. This is the power of the Holy Spirit which comes upon us when we crucify our flesh and receive the resurrection power (Holy Spirit) that raised Jesus from the dead.

Prayer is faith in the One who answers prayers

It takes faith to repent for our sins. By faith worlds were formed. Faith saw people raised from the dead. This is why it is so important to overcome the mountains of the senses as they hinder our relationship to the Father. Mountains of faith are hard to climb at times because the things we desire seem to be estranged from us. Hebrews 11:1 says, "Faith is the substance of things hoped for, the evidence of things not seen. If we want to see what faith can obtain for us we will have to amend our carnal ways as stated in Jeremiah 7:2-3.

2. Stand at the gate of the Lord's house and there proclaim this message. Hear the word of the Lord, all you people of Judah who come through these gates to worship the Lord.
3. This is what the Lord Almighty, the God of Israel, says: Reform your ways and your actions, and I will let you live in this place.

This message is not just for Israel. It is for all who desire to be with the Lord. We have to set our hearts to obey God as commanded in Ezra 7:10, "For Ezra had devoted himself to the study and observance of the Law of the Lord, and to teaching its decrees and laws in Israel."

Prayer presents choices

God has given man choices to make. He can continue on his pilgrimage with the Lord, making a highway for the Lord to come to him (prayer), or he can close his ears to the Lord's invitation to pray. Those who offer themselves willingly to God will rise up and learn God's ways and teach others His ways.

God will open our eyes to the tactics of the enemy if we give ourselves to Him. Just as God spoke to Ezra and Nehemiah when they began the work of rebuilding Jerusalem, so He will speak to those who journey with Him in prayer. God has not called us to walk in darkness and to grope like blind men. He has called us to walk in the light as He is the light of men. Let us rise to the brightness of His coming. "Arise, shine; for thy light is come, and the glory of the Lord is risen upon thee" (Isaiah 60:1).

God's spirit will reveal to us the path of life. He will take us to living waters and direct us into the glory of God so that we may know Him and the power of His resurrection. Turn to Philippians 3:10. "I want to know Christ and the power of His resurrection and the fellowship of sharing in His sufferings, becoming like Him in His death, and so, somehow, to attain to the resurrection from the dead."

Prayer involves experiencing resurrection power and sufferings

The soul can ache with grief in prayer and the body can feel exhausted or in pain. Each time we give ourselves to Him we obtain a greater dimension of His spirit. Prayer involves driving out the enemy from our land (spirit, soul, and body), and for others. We do this "little by little." It is a process. Even after great manifestations of God's presence our flesh still rises up to control. But, if we turn to the light or to His spirit, we will overcome and continue on in our fellowship with the Father.

God writes His laws on our hearts so that we can know Him and have the power to obey Him. He wrote the Ten Commandments on the tablets of stone and gave them to Moses. But the law couldn't make a person fellowship with God. Fellowship takes a "heart" attitude. When we prepare our hearts for God, we become a messenger of the Lord. We see this in Malachi 3:1-2:

1. See, I will send my messenger, who will prepare the way before me. Then suddenly the Lord you are seeking will come to his temple; the messenger of the covenant, whom you desire, will come, says the Lord Almighty.

2. But who can endure the day of his coming? Who can stand when he appears? For he will be like a refiner's fire or a launderer's soap.

3. He will sit as a refiner and purifier of silver; he will purify the Levites and refine them like gold and silver. Then the Lord will have men who will bring offerings in righteousness.

If God gives us an assignment and we wash our hands of it, (won't do it), then we fail to be a messenger of the Lord. Our voice for God will not be heard. Instead, our actions release a voice for the enemy to come and attack because we did not prepare our hearts for obedience. Psalm 19:3 says, "There is no speech or language where there is no voice heard." Without God's voice in a given situation, there will be a voice of destruction as shown in I John 1:1-4:

1. That which was from the beginning, which we have heard, which we have seen with our eyes, which we have looked at and our hands have touched—this we proclaim concerning the Word of life.
2. The life appeared: we have seen it and testify to it, and we proclaim to you the eternal life, which was with the Father and has appeared to us.
3. We proclaim to you what we have seen and heard, so that you also may have fellowship with us. And our fellowship is with the Father and with His son, Jesus Christ.
4. We write this to make our joy complete.

Notice verse 3. "We proclaim to you what we have seen and heard . . ." There are times that we pray for others without hearing how to pray, but there are times we are to "hear" how to pray and this is having spiritual authority. It is manifesting a revelation from God. Revelation means to take off the cover and to reveal to others what was previously not known. Revelation is God's disclosure or manifestation of Himself.

All revelations must line up with the Word

This is of the utmost importance! Many have been led astray from God by speaking a revelation which they have heard but which is contrary to the Word of God. This revelation was under the spirit of deception. Jeremiah 27:9 warns against listening to interpreters of dreams who prophesy from their soul and not from God's Word. He says they are lies to keep a person from obeying God.

Revelations are a voice to sound God's plans

When revelations come from people who are submitted to God, they will speak as from God. Each of us are to have a revelation of God's Word to us as we read the Word and understand it, or by the gifts of revelation given by the Holy Spirit. A revelation can be lost if it is not acted upon. James 2:24 says, "You see that a person is justified by what he does and not by faith alone." When a revelation is spoken, it needs to be meditated upon until the mind comprehends it and it becomes "quickened." All revelations from God come to the spirit in man first.

Revelations usher in future events

Revelations become a voice in prayer to usher in future events to be released at a "set time." Not all revelations are interpreted at the moment they are given as in the book of Revelation by John. There are also times that a revelation that is given before its time hardens the hearer's heart because of his lack of understanding.

Revelations need to be acted upon

There are times in which we will step out and respond to a revelation and then let go of it. The case of Peter who stepped out to walk on water and then saw the wind and became afraid is such a case. Peter saw Jesus walking on the water and heard the word, "Come." He stepped out of his "sense" knowledge and began walking on a revelation of Jesus, but when he became distracted, he lost the revelation of walking on water.

Revelations take us beyond the natural realm to help us possess the spiritual

Our senses are like our guardians to keep us until we are ready for a faith walk. This is emphasized in Galatians 3:23. "But before faith came, we were kept under guard by the law, kept for the faith which would afterward be revealed."

After a revelation comes faith to possess

Faith comes as a revelation to our spirits. It holds the key to the heavenly world. In order to be healed, we need a revelation of healing. Once revelation comes, sickness cannot bind. We will have the faith to step out like Peter. It says in Deut. 29:29, "The secret things belong to the Lord our God, but the things revealed belong to us and to our sons forever, that we may observe all the words of this law."

The God who said, "Let there be light," is the same God who reveals revelation light to our hearts. Once the light of Christ is revealed, then the glory of God will also be seen in us. Paul says in Colossians 2 that he prays that we understand the knowledge of God's mystery, that it is Christ in us the hope of glory. In Him are the treasures of wisdom and revelation. In Him the Father will be revealed so that we can worship God.

Prayer is a form of worship

Worship is the act of paying divine honors to a deity. Worship is expressed through prayers declaring who God is, what He has done, and what He will do. It is a divine encounter with God Himself. Just as worship is a service to God, so is prayer. There are times that we "put on prayer as a garment to enter into His presence. God has given us an example in Leviticus 8:

1. The Lord said to Moses,
2. Bring Aaron and his sons, their garments, the anointing oil, the bull for the sin offering, the two rams and the basket containing bread made without yeast.
3. and gather the entire assembly at the entrance to the Tent of Meeting.
4. Moses did as the Lord commanded him, and the assembly gathered as the Lord commanded him, and the assembly gathered at the entrance to the Tent of Meeting.
5. Moses said to the assembly, 'this is what the Lord commanded to be done.'
6. Then Moses brought Aaron and his sons forward and washed them with water.
7. He put the tunic on Aaron, tied the sash around him, clothed him with the robe and put the ephod on him. He also tied the ephod to him by its skillfully woven waistband so it was fastened on him.

After the meeting with Him was over, they were to take off that garment and put on one that was prepared to minister to man. When God's Spirit comes upon us for a specific type of prayer, say birthing intercession, when this type of prayer is over we do not continue to groan or stay in any bodily pain. There have been cases in which intercessors acted as if they were in prayer when there was not the garment of prayer on them. Their actions brought attention to themselves instead of bringing glory to God.

Just as these garments were a type of the garment of holiness, [robes that have been washed in the blood of the Lamb and the Word of God], prayers are to be in holiness to the Lord. We receive these assignments by putting off the old man with all of its lusts of the flesh, and put on Christ. Jesus is that garment.

There is another type of garment that we must look at. It is the garment of humility as seen in the story of Jonah, chapter 2, after he was swallowed by the large fish.

1.   From inside the fish Jonah prayed to he Lord his God.
2.   He said: 'In my distress I called to the Lord, and he answered me, from the depths of the grave I called for help, and you listened to my cry.'

Did you notice, God heard a sound coming from Jonah. It was the sound of true repentance for not honoring God's Word. It says in I Samuel 2:30 " . . . those who honor Me I will honor, but those who despise me will be disdained." When Jonah ran from the Lord, his actions were a voice of dishonor. How many times have we run from something God has told us to do? Did you even think that this was dishonoring God?

Chapter 2

Sounds From The Past, Present, And Future

Jesus as the Mediator between man and God sits at the right hand of God interceding for us on earth in three phases, the past, the present, and the future. Prayers in faith never die. Those making the prayers might be dead, but the spirit of the prayer speaks until they are fulfilled. "By faith Abel offered God a better sacrifice than Cain did. By faith he was commended as a righteous man, when God spoke well of his offerings. And by faith he still speaks, even though he is dead" (Hebrews 11:4).

Ordained festivals teach us about prayer

Each of the annual feasts ordained by God (found in Leviticus 23) are set to reveal God's plans on earth. We will look only at the feast of Passover at this time as it brings forth the truth of intercession in phases of time. There are three distinct parts to the Passover. The first stage emphasized the past by reminding us that God lead the Israelites out of Egypt. The second stage, the eating of the Passover meal, represents the present. The third stage, looking for the Messiah to come, represents the future when Jesus will return for His church.

Prayers call God to remembrance

Intercessors will be called upon to look at events in the past and call God to remembrance of certain things so that blessings can be released to the present. Intercessors will see the present and pray that God will change the things that are seen now to line up with God's future plans. Intercessors will also see things in the future to change the course of things seen so that they can either be diverted or received.

Intercessors are ministering saints

God's messengers on earth are much like the ministering angels in heaven. The angels work with our prayers to bring forth God's desired end in all three times, past, present, and future with one other element—judgment—which we will look at later when we speak on forensic intercession. But first, turn to Revelation 8:3-5:

3. Another angel, who had a golden censer, came and stood at the altar. He was given much incense to offer, with the prayers of all the saints, on the golden altar before the throne.
4. The smoke of the incense, together with the prayers of the saints, went up before God from the angel's hand.
5. Then the angel took the censer, filled it with fire from the altar, and hurled it on the earth; and there came peals of thunder, rumblings, flashes of lightning and an earthquake.

Another angel! This "another angel" is not Jesus, even though he stands as intercessor between God and the prayers of the saints. Chapters 5, 6, and 7 of Revelation clearly show this with the following comments:

Revelation 5: 9: You are worthy to take the scroll and to open its seals, because you were slain, and with your blood you purchased men for God from every tribe and language and people and nation. You have made them to be a kingdom and priests to serve our God, and they will reign on the earth.

Revelation 6:9-10. When he opened the fifth seal, I saw under the altar the souls of those who had been slain because of the word of God and the testimony they had maintained. They called out in a loud voice, 'How long, Sovereign Lord, holy and true, until you avenge our blood?'

Revelation 7:9-10: After this I looked and there before me was a great tribe, people and language, standing before the throne and in front of the Lamb. They were wearing white robes and were holding palm branches in their hands. And they cried out in a loud voice: 'Salvation belongs to our God, who sits on the throne, and to the Lamb.'

Those who pray stand in two positions

This "another angel" is seen as doing two specific functions. First, he takes the prayers of the saints mixed with the incense from the altar and presents them to God. Next, he takes the censer filled with fire and hurls it to the earth signifying judgment.

J. Vernon Mc Gee says that the "golden altar" is the place where prayer is offered. In the Old Testament, a pattern of the altar in heaven was placed in the tent by Moses to symbolize the prayers of the people rising toward heaven. It was a type of Jesus who would offer Himself as an incense of worship to God. It is "In His Name" that we pray to our heavenly Father going through Jesus, the golden altar.

These three areas can be seen as follows:

1. Those who died in faith and were taken to Abraham's bosom and ascended with Jesus when He arose. (Past).
2. Those who die in Christ today. (Present).
3. Those who remain alive when Christ returns. (Future).

We get a picture of the believers in the past, present, and the future in I Thessalonians 4:13-17:

> 13. Brothers, we do not want you to be ignorant about those who fall asleep, or to grieve like the rest of men, who have no hope.
> 14. we believe that Jesus died and rose again and so we believe that God will bring with Jesus those who have fallen asleep in him.
> 15. According to the Lord's own word, we tell you that we who are still alive, who are left till the coming of the Lord, will certainly not precede those who have fallen asleep.
> 16. For the Lord himself will come down from heaven, with a loud command, with the voice of the archangel and with the trumpet call of god, and the dead in Christ will rise first.
> 17. After that, we who are still alive and are left will be caught up together so we will be with the Lord forever.

Now there is a quandary, "What about those who die during the end time called "The Tribulation Period." There is also the Olam Haba which is the City of God coming down from heaven to join with those saved during the Messianic Reign on earth (Hebrews 11:18-19). If the future belongs to those waiting for the return of the Messiah, what comes after the future?

The future of the coming Messiah is in two distinctive parts. One is for the believers who escape natural death because of their faith in Christ, and those who are martyred for their faith in Christ at this time. I believe that this last phase of future events is where we will see forensic intercession in its fullest form coming from these. Turn to Revelation 6:9-10:

> 9. When he opened the fifth seal, I saw under the altar the souls of those who had been slain because of the word of God and the testimony they had maintained during the Messianic period.
>
> 10. They called out in a loud voice, "How long, Sovereign Lord, holy and true, until you judge the inhabitants of the earth and avenge our blood?

Those who were killed are actually asking God to judge those who killed them. And, it appears that He does, but with the judgment looks for those who will repent for their actions as seen in Malachi 4:

> 5. See, I will send you the prophet Elijah before that great and dreadful day of the Lord comes.
>
> 6. He will turn the hearts of the fathers to their children, and the hearts of the children to their fathers; or else I will come and strike the land with a curse.

Not everyone will heed our prayers

Revelation 9:20 tells us that not everyone will repent and turn to God. "The rest of mankind that were not killed by these plagues still did not repent of the work of their hands; they did not stop worshiping demons, and idols of gold, silver, bronze, stone and wood—idols that cannot see or hear or walk."

Prayers are a type of incense

Just as incense which rises beyond earth's gravitational pull into the presence of the Father, Psalm 141:1-2 says, "O Lord, I call to you; come quickly to me. Hear my voice when I call to you. May my prayer be set before you like incense; may the lifting up of my hands be like the evening sacrifice." There is power in prayer when we know the God of prayer and that He answers prayer. Look what Revelation 5:9-10 says,

9. You are worthy to take the scroll and to open its seals, because you were slain, and with our blood you purchased men for God from every tribe and language and people and nation.

10. You have made them to be a kingdom and priests to serve our God, and they will reign on the earth.

Prayers are a type of firstfruit offerings

Firstfruit offerings are made in faith that our prayers will ascend to the Father and that the Lord Jesus will mediate these prayers, and that we can expect answers and blessings regarding these prayers. The Illustrated Davis Dictionary of the Bible says, "The fruits first ripe was an earnest of the coming harvest." Firstfruits were to be given as an offering to Jehovah on behalf of nations, people, and situations.

"I have faith that You, Lord, will bless this harvest before I see it." "I honor You as the "Firstfruit". Remember, Jesus was the Firstborn, the Firstfruit of redemption.

Prayers that affect future generations

Romans 8:29 says, "For from the very beginning God decided that those who came to him—and all along he knew who would—should become like his Son, so that his Son would be the first, with many brothers." And in Romans 11:16, "And since Abraham and the prophets are God's people, their children will be too. For if the roots of the tree are holy, the branches will be too."

When we offer the firstfruits to God and He accepts it as a holy offering, the rest of the harvest will be holy. Sometimes we need a visual lesson from earthly things so that when we look into the New Testament and see that we are to be holy because Jesus is holy. And we are of His Seed! Then, each time we observe the Festival of the Firstfruits we can have faith that God is accepting us because of His Son and that He will provide for our needs, spirit, soul, and body.

Prayers act as arbitration

Revelation 8 speaks of the judgments as seen in the fire from the altar being hurled to the earth. Jesus judges sin, and because we are of His seed, we are to judge after His judgments. This type of judgment is called *forensic intercession*. Let's look at Psalm 63:9-10 to see how David decided against those who sought his life:

9. They who seek my life will be destroyed; they will go down to the depths of the earth.

10. They will be given over to the sword and become food for jackals.

David did not act presumptuously with this decree. When you read the rest of Psalm 63, you will find out that he has seen God in the sanctuary and beheld His power and His glory. He experienced His love and knew His name. Praise of God was in his heart and on his lips. David did not speak against his enemies from any hurt within his heart. He spoke prophetically at the time of judgment. In this psalm we see that an enemy came to take David's life from him which God had not sent. Therefore, David spoke to the evil prophetically just as he did in Psalm 22 when he spoke as if he were the one on the cross. The following are incidences of *forensic intercession:*

In *forensic intercession* we will bring to court before the living judge of heaven evidence for and against Satan's claim to take someone's land. (This is a type of the incense rising toward heaven in Revelation 8). We are to be as God's representatives on earth allowing His will and ways to come forth and through us. But! Jeremiah 10:21 says that God has something against us, "The pastors are become brutish, and have not sought the Lord: therefore they shall not prosper, and all their flock is scattered."

The shepherds are called to get God's word for any type of arbitration that is needed—and that includes intercessors. As intercessors, we will become brute beasts if we fight the enemy without the judgments of God. When David spoke to those seeking his life he knew the word, "Touch not mine anointed." David lived the Word in obedience as seen in his actions with King Saul.

To help us understand this type of intercession, we need to define the word *forensic*. It means suitable for public debate, characteristics of law, spoken or written exercise in argumentation. To get a better understanding of the term argumentation, we need to first look at Job 1:6-8:

6. One day the angels came to present themselves before the Lord, and Satan also came with them.

7. The Lord said to Satan, 'Where have you come from'? Satan answered the Lord, from roaming through the earth and going back and forth in it.

8. Then the Lord said to Satan, Have you considered my servant Job? There is no one on earth like him; he is blameless and upright, a man who fears God and *shuns* evil.

Satan was arguing with God saying that Job loved God because of the hedge God had placed around him. God, on the other hand, states that Job shunned evil because he was righteous. After presenting his arguments, God decides to remove the hedge placed around Job. Verses 9-12 reveal Satan's arguments and God's decision:

9. Does Job fear God for nothing? Satan replied.
10. Have you not put a hedge around him and his household and everything he has? You have blessed the work of his hands, so that his flocks and herds are spread throughout the land.
11. But stretch out your hand and strike everything he has, and he will surely curse you to your face.
12. The Lord said to Satan, Very well, then, everything he has is in your hands, but on the man himself do not lay a finger.

Satan accuses God and man

Satan was accusing God of using His power to protect Job unlawfully (Job feared that his children would sin against God in their drunken banquets). In Revelation 12:10 Satan is called the accuser of the brethren. Satan not only accuses us when we sin against God, but accused God Himself of false protection. The word *accuser* in the Greek means to be a plaintiff, to charge someone with an offense against one in the compliance of law.

Satan doesn't have to lie to God about us

There is a High Court in Heaven and God is the Judge. Satan comes with accusations regarding us in accordance with the laws of God. Evidence is being set forth on both sides. Satan presents his case which will always be accurate of the offense. Satan does not need lie to God, our actions witness against us. Satan just reminds God of something that either we did or according to a "voice" of a previous act done in our genealogy. Satan calls as witnesses against us "the voices of reason," "the voices of doubt" and the "voices of pride."

God does not make His judgments on the accusations against us, but on whether we have applied the blood of His Son to our hearts. His judgments only comes after all intercession has been completed and we have been given ample time to repent. God did not judge those who came out of Egypt until their iniquity was complete. In fact, intercession was released in three stages:

while they were in Egypt, while they were in the wilderness, and when He gave them their inheritance in the land of Canaan.

We can identify with the Israelites in three ways:

1. Before salvation, we "live in Egypt" even though were being beckoned by the Holy Spirit.
2. We are in the desert spiritually when we continue living in our flesh after accepting Jesus as our Savior.
3. And when we cross over; we walk in the spirit.

Knowing is not always possessing

Knowing God's plans for us is no guarantee that we will possess these plans. We need to look at what happened to Israel to teach us the art of driving out the enemies who confront us. While the Israelites were in Egypt, tenants worked the land which was given as a possession to the Israelites. Now, the original owners are coming back to take up residence and evict the tenants. The tenants won't like this and unless shown legal reasons for them to leave, they won't.

What we are to learn from this is, our old nature held possession of our spirits, minds, and bodies. Just asking Jesus into our hearts has not changed that. All that has changed is Jesus who defeated our enemies will be there for us if we turn to Him and deny self. There will be just as much a battle for us as there was for the Israelites. By looking at their mistakes, we can learn what to do and what not to do—if we will listen to the voices of the past.

By looking at the life of Moses, we can learn to sanctify God amongst the people we live with. Without sanctification we will not inherit God's plans. Moses was a great leader, but, God required more of him than just leading a people.

If we doubt that God will have a place for us to settle in, we need to look at the time when God divided up the land of Canaan and gave each tribe a possession. When God gives us our possessions, He will set limits for us to follow as seen in Deuteronomy 32:8. "When the Most High divided to the nations their inheritance, when he separated the sons of Adam, he set the bounds of the people according to the number of the children of Israel."

Prayer is possessing

God will not give us more than we are able to take possession of and hold by His Spirit. We decide our blessings according to the degree hat we are able to subdue our flesh. God is waiting on us!

Notice, there is a time appointed by God in which He divides up our inheritance and sets the bounds to reconcile accounts as in Matthew 18:23-27:

23. Therefore, the kingdom of heaven is like a king who wanted to settle accounts with his servants.
24. As he began the settlement, a man who owed him ten thousand talents was brought to him.
25. since he was not able to pay, the master ordered that he and his wife and his children and all that he had be sold to repay the debt.
26. The servant fell on his knees before him. 'Be patient with me,' he begged, 'and I will pay back everything.'
27. The servant's master took pity on him, canceled the debt and let him go.

As long as we hold onto our flesh, we let go of our inheritance. God is waiting on us to release all bitterness and unforgiveness from our hearts toward those who have hurt us. Another example is found in Matthew 19:28-30:

28. I tell you the truth, at the renewal of all things, when the Son of Man sits on his glorious throne, you who have followed me will also sit on twelve thrones, judging the twelve tribes of Israel.
29. And everyone who has left houses or brothers or sisters or father or mother or children or fields for my sake will receive a hundred times as much and will inherit eternal life.

These examples are placed here for us to see the value of knowing God's plans to bless us. He has so much in store for us, waiting until we make our enemies our footstools. To obtain these promises, we need to learn intercession for ourselves and to help our brothers and sisters to obtain their inheritances.

Prayer binds and loosens

When God uses us in forensic intercession, we bind and loose according to Matthew 18:18 which clearly tells us that we are to pray according to the plan in heaven for that individual. We cannot pray something for someone that God has not given to them. This would be foolish, for if they are not equipped to hold their land they will lose it, become discouraged, and blame God. We need to be very careful in our prayers. To pray that someone becomes a millionaire when he has not learned to tithe invites devastation. To pray that someone becomes a carpenter when he desires to be a musician is likewise foolish. Ecclesiastes 5 instructs us with this advice:

1. Guard your steps when you go to the house of God. Go near to listen rather than to offer the sacrifice of fools, who do not know that they do wrong.
2. Do not be quick with your mouth, do not be hasty in your heart to utter anything before God. God is in heaven and you are on earth, so let your words be few.
3. As a dream comes when there are many cares, so the speech of a fool when there are many words.
4. When you make a vow to God, do not delay in fulfilling it. He has no pleasure in fools; fulfill your vow.
5. It is better not to vow than to make a vow and not fulfill it.

Matthew 18 spoke on binding and loosening. by speaking words. Each time we speak God's Word over a situation, we either bind the enemy or loose that one held by the enemy. We also bind God's blessings coming to us by negative words, false words, or words in the form of a vow. Words have a voice to declare obedience or disobedience. We will look at a vow given presumptuously in the story of Ananias and Sapphira in Acts 5.

Ananias and Sapphira made a vow to give a certain amount of money to the apostles to help others. However, when their land was sold, they held back part of the price. Peter knew by the Holy Spirit that they lied! He immediately corrected them. Peter said in verse 3, " . . . how it is that Satan has so filled your heart that you have lied to the Holy Spirit and have kept for yourself some of the money you received for the land?" When Ananiah heard these words, he fell down dead. Judgment came harshly. Vows to God are that important. They are debts owed to Him.

If we do not pay our debts whether they are to man or to God, we will be held in bondage until the debt is paid. Just as God gives us the power to get the wealth, He gives us the power to keep our vows or power to release our vows through repentance. We can make a vow from our emotions instead of from our spirit. When this happens, we are bound to our lower nature.

Prayers are vows to God

Emotional vows bind us to a sentence of death as they are under the curse. Only God can break these vows and set us free. Vows are a type of covenant. They are words which we make as a promise. Vows from our flesh are under the spirit of pride. They are places we run to for refuge instead of God. Let's see what God says about them in Isaiah 28:15-19:

> 15. You boast, 'We have entered into a covenant with death, with the grave we have made an agreement. When an overwhelming scourge sweeps by, for we have made a lie our refuge and falsehood our hiding place.'
> 16. So this is what the Sovereign Lord says: 'See, I lay a stone in Zion, a tested stone, a precious cornerstone for a sure foundation.
> 17. I will make justice the measuring line and righteousness the plumb line; hail will sweep away your refuge, the lie, and water will overflow your hiding place.
> 18. Your covenant with death will be annulled; your agreement with the grave will not stand.'

God wants to redeem us and to restore us to fellowship with Him. To do this we have to see how we have bound ourselves to our flesh, which allows the enemy to steal from us. When our eyes are opened to see what we have made our god and choose God instead, our life is prolonged. Deuteronomy 30:17-18 says,

> 17. But if your heart turns away and you are not obedient, and if you are drawn away to bow down to other gods and worship them,
> 18. I declare to you this day that you will certainly be destroyed. You will not live long in the land you are crossing the Jordan to enter and possess.

God's words, spoken years before Ananias and Sapphira were even born spoke as a testimony to their choice of choosing wealth and recognition as their god. They had forgotten the word of the Lord as we continue to read:

19. This day I choose heaven and earth as witnesses against you
    that I have set before you life and death, blessings and curses.
    Now choose life, so that you and your children may live
20. and that you may love the Lord your God, listen to his voice,
    and hold fast to him.

Prayer can prolong life

It is not a vain thing for us to choose obedience to God. It is our life, and through this thing we shall prolong our days in the land. Notice, "Prolong your days." God does say that there are set times for us, but also that our days can either be cut short or prolonged depending on our faithfulness to Him and our choices. Hosea 14:9 asks, "Who is wise? He will realize these things. Who is discerning? He will understand them. The ways of the Lord are right; the righteous walk in them, but the rebellious stumble in them."

The ways of God are just. When Ananias and Sapphira died, it was because of the choice to disregard God's Word. They did not know God's character or nature to fulfill His words. God did not punish them because He was angry with them. God let their hearts judge their actions. We have to know that God is good all of the time. David knew God to be just from the following psalm that he wrote. He said, "The Lord is upright; he is my Rock, and there is no wickedness in him" (Psalm 92:15). When God makes a judgment, it will not be because of any wickedness in Him, only fairness.

A new work was being done after the outpouring of the Holy Spirit. Church was born in a day and God could not allow it to be destroyed because of sin. Sin keeps the land under the curse that Jesus came to redeem. If repentance is not seen, the land (the church) is hindered from producing its best. So, we ought to listen to the message the story of Ananias and Sapphira has for us—be careful what we promise to God!

The enemy prays

There is another voice which cries out from the past, only this voice cries vengeance instead of intercession. In Genesis 4:10-12 we read that blood is crying out.

10. And the Lord said, 'what have you done? The voice of your
    brother's blood is crying to me from the ground.

11. And now you are cursed from the ground, which has opened its mouth to receive your brother's blood from your hand.
12. When you till the ground, it shall no longer yield to you its strength.

The word "cry" in Hebrews, (using the Strong's Concordance) means means "proclaim by shriek." The land and all that God created, was meant to cry "glory and honor and praise" to God. The land was meant to give itself to the increase of man, but blood guilt or innocent blood upon the land stopped the blessings from coming forth just as broken vows can do. There is only one way to stop the voice of blood, it is through the act of restoration. Jesus came to restore us back to the Father and stop the cry for our blood. But what about the cry for justice when an injustice was committed?

Prayer is used to repent for injustice

The United States had made treaties with the American Indians years ago and then broke their word. There have been similar vows broken by our government, which opened the door for the enemy to come to our nation. Many intercessors have repented for the injustices, but something more had to be done. For many of these, a court settlement was made and a certain amount of monies were paid to the injured parties. God listens to the vows of individuals as well as the vows a nation makes and releases intercessors to hear the voice of injustice. We need to cry out to God to release the laborers into the fields of prayer as seen in Psalm 61:

1. Hear my cry, O God; listen to my prayer.
2. From the ends of the earth I call to you, I call as my heart grows faint; lead me to the rock that is higher than I.
3. For you have been my refuge, a strong tower against the foe.
4. I long to dwell in your tent forever and take refuge in the shelter of your wings.
5. For you have heard my vows, O God, you have given me the heritage of those who fear your name.
6. Increase the days of the king's life, his years for many generations.
7. May he be enthroned in God's presence forever; appoint your love and faithfulness to protect him.
8. Then will I ever sing praise to your name and fulfill my vows day after day.

Because David fulfilled his vows to God, he had a right to ask God for the blessings. David wanted his heritage and so should we. The dictionary says that heritage is that which comes or belongs to one by reason of birth; an inherited lot or portion; something reserved for one that which has been or may be inherited by legal descent or succession. It is the land apportioned to us by right of inheritance.

King David, prior to his crowning, experienced his heritage taken from him by the Amalekites in I Samuel 30:6-8. They came to Ziklag, burned it with fire, and took all the women captive, (Including David's two wives).

6.   And David was greatly distressed; for the people spake of stoning him, because the soul of all the people was grieved, every man for his sons and for his daughters: but David encouraged himself in the Lord his God.

7.   And David said to Abiathar the priest, Ahimelech's son, I pray thee, bring me hither the ephod. And Abiathar brought thither the ephod to David.

8.   And David inquired of the Lord, saying, 'Shall I pursue after this troop? Will I overtake them?' 'Pursue them,' he answered. 'You will certainly overtake them and succeed in the rescue.'

When we recognize what the enemy has stolen from us, like David we should cry out to God for the intercession needed to fight the battle required to pull down the strongholds of darkness.

Psalm 53 tells us that those who do not seek God when the enemy comes are corrupt. The enemy comes to take our inheritance. We will only get it back if we seek God's salvation for the situation. If we do not, shame comes instead. The shame is seen in "not" receiving back the things which the enemy stole from us.

John 3:27 says, "A man can receive nothing except it be given him from heaven." Unless we seek Him, we will not receive from Him. "Oh, that salvation for Israel would come out of Zion!" (Psalm 63:6). We are spiritual Israel. Our cry should be, "Lord, let your intercession come from within us!"

Prayer is our covenant right

We have a covenant with God which means He is to fight for us when we are attacked. This fight involves angels ministering to us and against our enemies. It involves others praying for God's intervention in our lives. And, it involves our praying under spiritual authority. This covenant, however, is conditional and unconditional. God will not come upon us in spiritual intercession while we are in sin. Our hearts have to be right with Him. There are those who have lost their rights and their heritage because of:

Not knowing their rights to ask God's help.
Not repenting for known sins.
Not having the knowledge needed.
Not separating themselves from demonic activity.

When we choose to obey His Word, then according to Ezekiel 36:27 " . . . I will put My Spirit within you and cause you to walk in My statutes, and you will be careful to observe My ordinances." Any failure in obtaining our heritage is a failure on our part and not on God's. It will be a failure to not observe one of God's laws.

God will take us back to these times by allowing another situation to arise which is similar to the situation we failed to overcome with the word. When we overcome, we are in readiness to be used by God to pray for others who are in the same situation we were in.

An example of this can be as follows: suppose you are tempted to steal and you succumb to the temptation. After being convicted by the Holy Spirit, you repent for your actions and determine not to steal again. Years might pass when another opportunity comes for you to steal. But, remembering how sorry you felt for sinning against God, you confront the temptation with the Word and refuse the temptation. Now you are ready to be used by God to pray for others who are tempted to steal. Because you have overcome, you have gained territory, so to speak.

For David, one of his inheritances was his two wives. He had a legal right to get them back, but still he had to ask God for the power and authority to do it. God has given to each of us something to inherit and possess. As we seek Him, He will reveal to us what that land is. He will also use us in intercession to help others receive back their inheritance, even if it has been lost for several generations.

There is an inheritance which we have lost that most of us never even considered as an inheritance. It is the right to loath ourselves for the sins we have committed. Turn to Ezekiel 36:30-31:

30.   I will increase the fruit of the trees and the crops of the field,
      so that you will no longer suffer disgrace among the nations
      because of famine.

31.   Then you will remember your evil ways and wicked deeds, and you will loathe yourselves for your sins and detestable practices.

This gift is so that we will not tolerate sin in our members. Our loathing will be a voice to God that we are truly repentant.

Repentance is our inheritance

God is looking for opportunities to gain access into the lives of man on earth. He needs vessels that will hear His voice and respond. The first response that we are to have is to submit the gifts He gives us to His Spirit. We can operate the gifts in our flesh, but we will not enter His Kingdom if we do. Regarding speaking or praying in tongues, we can use this gift of God in our flesh. If we do, we will not have spiritual authority to take anything back from Satan. It is written that in times past God winked at our disobedience, but now that He is teaching us, He expects us to learn how to wait upon His Spirit to pray. God will test our motives and actions much like He did Job. The testing is not to destroy us, but to cause increase in all that God gives to us.

Increase is seen when we are able to pray successfully for others to be redeemed. Galatians 6:1 says, "Brothers, if someone is caught in a sin, you who are spiritual should restore him." Notice the word spiritual. Being spiritual is praying in the spirit, not out of anger or fear. We will be tested as to our motives for interceding. Intercessors can pray with an attitude of superiority as well as feelings of inferiority. As we continue on with the Lord, we will learn how to hear the voice of God when He wants us to pray. In Psalm 138:8, we are told that the Lord will not abandon the works of His hands. When God asks us to pray, He will see to it that the prayer is completed.

Prayer is intercession invoking our covenant with God, from God, and by His Spirit using us

When we leave off communicating with Him and attempt to intercede or pray without Him, we create from our lower nature and have broken covenant with Him. This work will eventually be led to destruction. There will be times that we need to examine ourselves. Are we bringing forth His fruit or just blowing hot air?

Spiritual Intercession brings forth fruit

Much like a farmer works to bring forth a harvest, those who pray work for the same reward. There is an appointed time for harvest. It might not be in our lifetime, but it will produce according to God's appointed time.

Prayers can be rushed

Even though there is an appointed time for harvest, we can try to rush harvest time. If we pick too soon, the fruit can be thrown away and we will not receive a financial reward. We can try to bring forth something to maturity before its time only to lose everything and have to start over.

Intercessors can be seduced to pray

Situations can arise in which we hate the offense and begin to intercede out of anger. Sometimes we need to ask ourselves why we are interceding for someone. James 1:20 tells us that man's anger will not do anything righteous with God.

Intercession will be judged by God

Intercession is as much a work as hoeing weeds. It will be judged by the blood and by fire. If the intercession produced fruit, the fruit will remain. If not, we suffer loss. Only that which passes through the blood will receive a reward. All else is burned as by fire.

God's hand upholds the work of His hands, but He destroys the works of our hands. When we intercede in His Spirit, our words will go forth to create, sustain, or destroy. Isaiah 58:12 speaks of the time of repair and restoration. "Your people will rebuild the ancient ruins and will raise up the age-old foundations; you will be called Repairer of Broken Walls, Restorer of Streets with Dwellings." When the intercession is from God, then that which He wants restored will be restored.

Intercession builds and restores

It is not enough to tear down the false images, strongholds, and walls which prevent people from receiving from God. God is a God of restoration.

He restores people, positions, and buildings. The following is an example of God restoring someone Satan had taken captive in Zechariah 3.

1. Then He showed me Joshua the high priest standing before the angel of the Lord.
2. The Lord said to Satan, 'The Lord rebuke you, Satan! The Lord, who has chosen Jerusalem, rebuke you!' Is not this man a burning stick snatched from the fire?
3. Now Joshua was dressed in filthy clothes as he stood before the angel.
4. The angel said to those who were standing before him, Take off his filthy clothes. Then he said to Joshua, See, I have taken away your sin, and I will put rich garments on you.
5. Then I said, 'Put a clean turban on his head' So they put a clean turban on his head and clothed him, while the angel of the Lord stood by.
6. The angel of the Lord gave this charge to Joshua:
7. This is what the Lord Almighty says: 'If you will walk in my ways and keep my requirements, then you will govern my house and have charge of my courts, and I will give you a place among these standing here.'

God did not leave Joshua naked. Yes, he had his filthy garments removed, but then he had new garments placed on him as well as a turban for his head. God will not leave us in the shame and guilt of our sins, either. He clothes us in His righteousness and His glory to represent Him once again. Unless we have the Lord remove our filth and anoint us with His word, we will not be able to conduct business after His Spirit. Look at the following scriptures:

Acts 1:8. You will receive power when the Holy Spirit comes on you and you will be My witnesses.

I John 1:1. That which was from the beginning which we have heard, which we have seen with our eyes, which we have looked at and our hands have touched—this we proclaim concerning the Word of life.

Isaiah 55:3-4. I will make an everlasting covenant with you, my faithful love promised to David. See, I have made him a witness to the peoples, a leader and commander of the peoples.

Acts 13:34. I will give you the holy and sure blessings promised to David. (This is speaking of Jesus and to His seed).

This covenant of David is for us to wear the garments of kings and priests to judge righteously. Isaiah 41:1 tells us that the whole world is moving toward judgment. If the dirty garments were allowed to remain on us, we would be taken back in remembrance of our sins and return to them instead of staying in God's Word.

> Romans 1:9. God, whom I serve with my whole heart in preaching the gospel of his Son, is my witness how constantly I remember you.

> Hebrews 2:4. God also testified to it by signs, wonders, and various miracles, and gifts of the Holy Spirit distributed according to his will.

> Revelation 1:5, Christ, who is the faithful witness, will be there at your court date.

> Hebrews 10:15, The Holy Spirit bears witness.

There will be another witness: either our faithfulness or our iniquities. James 5:3-4 says,

3. Your gold and silver are corroded. Their corrosion will testify against you and eat your flesh like fire. You have hoarded wealth in the last days.
4. Look! The wages you failed to pay the workmen who mowed your fields are crying out against you.

Those who have died before us will also be a witness for/against us as seen in Hebrews 12:1. "Therefore, since we are surrounded by such a great cloud of witnesses, let us throw off everything that hinders and the sin that so easily entangles, and let us run with perseverance the race marked out for us."

Times of prayer

a. When God's Word needs to be sent.
b. When the soul needs to be crucified. (Psalm 22).

c. When power is needed by the Holy Spirit. (Acts 13:34).
d. When authority needs to be exercised over darkness. (II Corinthians 10:3-6).

Intercessors have the spirit of fear of God

Psalm 128 represents the person who fears the Lord—he eats the fruit of his labor, blessings and prosperity are his, his wife is fruitful, and his sons are like olive shoots. The olive tree represents prosperity, divine blessings, beauty and strength. Additional scriptures are Psalm 52:8, Jeremiah 11:16, and Hosea 14:6).

Reasons for intercession can be hidden from the intercessor

Mysteries belong to God. He is not obligated to reveal to us why we are interceding. There will be times that the Spirit comes upon us and we lack the knowledge of the intercession. We can pray for individuals in foreign countries and for countries without our knowing it. Deut. 29:29 says, "The secret things belong to the Lord our God, but the things revealed belong to us and to our children forever, that we may follow all the words of the law." The Holy Spirit brings light and revelation to the Word of God if and when He wants us to know something. Until then, we just yield ourselves to His Spirit.

Intercessors pray for Israel

We are told to pray for the peace of Jerusalem. Praying for Israel is a response of love. In Psalm 122:6 it says, "May those who love you be secure." Love released has its rewards. Those who pray for Israel receive special blessings from God

Intercessors can be spiritual mothers

Looking back in history to Judges 5:7, 12, we read, "I, Deborah, arose a mother in Israel." Deborah was a prophet to Israel who carried Israel spiritually. Paul represented being a spiritual mother to Onesimus. A spiritual mother holds God's Word for someone until it can be seen in the person or in the case of Deborah, a nation. This person is used to teach and train others in Christ until they are formed into His image. (Galatians 4:19).

They are called mothers of Zion because they labor and travail for souls to come out of darkness into the light of Christ. These intercede not only to bring forth a people out of darkness, but into His plans. They help to prepare a people to know the purpose of God for their lives so that they can serve Him in His kingdom.

Intercessors carry others with a power given to them by God. This power is called the virtue of God. The root word of virtue means to dance, whirl, travail, or bring forth.

The thought of "spiritual pregnancy is seen in Psalm 29:8, "The voice of the Lord shakes the wilderness." "Shake" in Hebrew is the word *Chuwl* which means travail, birth pangs, and to give birth. Zion "gave birth" to a nation as seen in Isaiah 66:

> 7. Before she goes into labor, she gives birth; before the pains come upon her, she delivers a son.
> 8. Who has ever heard of such a thing? Who has ever seen such things? Can a country be born in a day or a nation be brought forth in a moment? Yet no sooner is Zion in labor than she gives birth to her children.
> 9. Do I bring to the moment of birth and not give delivery? Says the Lord. Do I close up the womb when I bring to delivery? Says your God.

Birthing was a good work created in the intercessor being used as Christ for others to do. Ephesians 2:10 says, "For we are God's workmanship, created in Christ Jesus to do good works, which God prepared in advance for us to do."

Mary gave her body to be used by the Holy Spirit to bring forth the "physical" Christ. In like manner we yield our bodies to bring forth spiritual Christ in His sons and daughters. Spiritual mothers carry the plans of God for others. "For who among men knows the thoughts of a man except the man's spirit within him?" (I Cor. 2:11).

Mothers needed for Backsliders

Backsliders become strangers to the covenant of promise and lose their hope of eternal blessings. God, in His mercy, gives hope to one who knows his covenant and can carry the backslider until he comes to his senses.

Proverbs 14:14 says a backslider in heart does his own way. A person who does his own way is a stranger to God and needs to be birthed into the kingdom of God. John 3:3 says, "Unless a man is born again, he cannot see the kingdom of God." It takes spiritual birthing for others to receive Jesus as Lord. Nothing spiritual comes into this world unless it is birthed in prayer.

Intercessors can experience a miscarrying womb

A miscarrying womb for an intercessor is when he or she has begun intercession but fails to complete it usually because he or she has become upset with the person they are holding in prayer or begins to believe that their prayers are vain for this person. When this happens, God will call upon someone else to intercede or re-give us the assignment at a later date. Paul was even concerned that his labor would be in vain. I Thessalonians 3:5 tells us that the tempter tempts us to not give ourselves to intercede or birth others into the kingdom.

From conception to delivery is a span of time called trimesters. In each trimester we experience different manifestations much like those of a woman bringing forth natural children. In the first trimester, when conception has occurred, preparation is made for sanctification. In this first stage, the person receiving the Word of God feels joy and happiness over the Word.

In the second trimester, the person accepts the changes that seem to occur within her/him and their surroundings. They have come into agreement with the Word and establish a covenant of promise with God. Visible changes are now seen by others.

In the third trimester, focus is needed for completion. Satan comes to tempt and to try the Word given so that it can be aborted. He releases fear, words of failure, doubt, and panic attacks through oppression. We begin to ask ourselves, "Do I even want that which the Word promises me?" Thoughts of having a spiritual abortion come, and strong urges to quit are present. Our continued perseverance in prayer identifies our love for God. Turn to II Corinthians 1:3-7:

3. Praise be to the God and Father of our Lord Jesus Christ, the Father of compassion and the God of all comfort.
4. who comforts us in all our troubles, so that we can comfort those in any trouble with the comfort we ourselves have received from God.
5. For just as the sufferings of Christ flow over into our lives, so also through Christ our comfort overflows.
6. If we are distressed, it is for your comfort and salvation; if we are comforted, it is for your comfort, which produces in you patient endurance of the same sufferings we suffer.

7.   And our hope for you is firm, because we know that just as
      you share in our sufferings, so also you share in our comfort.

Intercessors suffer spiritually, physically and emotionally

There is a suffering in intercession, but the rewards outweigh any long-lasting regrets. God does not take joy in seeing people perish. He is a God of love and wants all to be saved. Revelation 1:9 says, "I, John, our brother and companion in the suffering and kingdom and patient endurance that are ours in Jesus, was on the island of Patmos because of the word of God and the testimony of Jesus." God will always raise up someone to stand with a Christian who is suffering because of the Word. We might not know who it is, but he is there in intercession because of God's faithfulness not to leave us alone. Will you be that one that God will use?

Intercessors receive crowns

God gives all of His children crowns. Crowns represent authority. Our authority must be laid down at the feet of Him who sits on the throne. We must worship Him and give Him all the glory and honor. When we are in a place of defeat, we are not worshipping God. When we continue meditating on the bad things which have happened, Satan gets the glory. God came to bless us in many ways, but the most important way is this, to be able to worship Him with a pure heart of thanksgiving and honor to Him. Revelation 25:11 says, "But Lord, my sins! How many they are. Oh, pardon them for the honor of your name."

Whenever we go to God and repent for our sins, though they are many, we bring honor to Him who sits on the throne. It goes on to say that then He will direct our path, we will live in the circle of His blessings, and our children shall inherit the earth.

God's plan for our lives is only revealed when we welcome His authority. This usually comes after judgment for sins! After judgment comes peace and then restoration.

Intercessors receive supernatural strength

God will be a source of strength to those who turn back the battle at the gate. He will be a spirit of justice to him who sits in judgment. He will make justice the measuring line and righteousness the plumb line. He will instruct and teach those who want to be His instruments. It is the Lord Almighty, wonderful in counsel and magnificent in wisdom that does these things. Let us praise His holy name! (Taken from Isaiah 28)

Intercessors deliver others from captivity

God is a righteous God, and, as such, He must punish unrighteousness. Those who are taken into captivity because of their unrighteousness are not left without. Intercessors are raised up to comfort and correct. These "cry" out to God for mercy so that they can be led out of captivity.

Jesus gives us the example of leading those held in the captivity of Abraham's bosom in Ephesians 4:8. Jesus led these out of the place they were kept into the presence of the Father in heaven. "When he ascended on high, he led captives in his train and gave gifts to men." He was able to lead a people to their ascension because He descended or went to the place where those in captivity were held.

Paul tells us in Romans 9:3 that he would gladly feel the separation from the presence of God for the sake of his brethren. He was willing to go to the places of darkness that they lived in to be able to lead them to the light.

Chapter 3

Prayers of Restoration

An example of an intercessor seeing the present, past, and future is seen in the story of Philemon. Paul was such an intercessor. He knew where Philemon was spiritually what he could be in Jesus, and what he was to his master.

In the story of Philemon, we see Paul speak, as it were, to Philemon on behalf of Onesimus, a runaway slave.

Onesimus' name means useful, helpful, practical, functional, of use, constructive, positive, valuable, and handy. Onesimus escapes from his master and runs away to Rome where he hears Paul preach about the saving grace of Jesus Christ, which gave Onesimus hope. Somehow, they made acquaintance and Paul and Onesimus became good friends. Paul saw the usefulness in Onesimus and his gift to be of help.

When we pray to God either for ourselves or for others, we have to see the value in us and in others. If all we see are the things we hate about ourselves, we will not be able to make the exchange God has for us. We are worthy to receive help in time of need because Jesus is worthy and we are in Him. Paul was able to go beyond seeing Onesimus as a slave to a person of worth.

Paul saw Onesimus as one "to be helpful or useful" to his master. He saw that this gift was in bondage, yes, but knew that his prayers would become effectual to change the relationship between master and slave. He not only prays for both of them, but writes a letter to Philemon urging him to receive Onesimus as Paul, himself. Paul had been very helpful to Philemon, so for Paul to state that Philemon should receive Onesimus as Paul was asking a great deal.

Each of us is a slave to our lower nature, and the God-given gifts in us need to be set free. God uses people to pray for us for this to happen just as He used Paul. Paul knew that we were with the Father before creation (Ephesians 1:4), and that the only way to unlock God's plan was to offer prayers to the Father on another's behalf. Paul was able to see beyond the earthly offense (that

Onesimus wasn't helpful to his master) to see his spiritual gift of helpfulness. We are to do the same with those God brings to us.

God wants to be touched by man. Jesus said that He is touched with our infirmities. God came to the Garden of Eden to "touch" Adam and Eve. When we run away from God, He uses people to reconcile us back to Himself. Paul saw something of the Christ in Onesimus. He saw his usefulness as a brother, which was of more value than his usefulness as a slave. We have been called to serve God, but God wants our service to Him out of a relationship of brotherhood through Jesus Christ.

Let the Walls Come Down

Intercessors being used under the authority of the Holy Spirit tear down walls that have stood for centuries to keep us from that which rightly belongs to us. We will look at different ways walls can come down to see things that are rightly ours.

When we serve God and obey Him through love, then we have certain promises available to us. I Peter 4:8, "Above all, love each other deeply, because love covers over a multitude of sins." Sometimes, I think, we take this promise much too lightly. We must understand that God's Word comes with power and manifestations of reward. Turn to II Samuel 2:4-7:

4. When David was told that it was the men of Jabesh Gilead who had buried Saul,
5. he sent messengers to the men of Jabesh Gilead to say to them, 'The Lord bless you for showing this kindness to Saul your master by burying him.
6. May the Lord now show you kindness and faithfulness, and I too will show you the same favor because you have done this.
7. Now then, be strong and brave, for Saul your master is dead, and the house of Judah has anointed me king over them.'

Charity causes walls to fall

The word favor means kindness, grace, pleasant, and precious. When we sow charity, which is God's love and kindness, we come under the law of sowing and reaping of that which we have sowed. If we seem to be born with a silver spoon in our mouth, then one of our ancestor's sowed charity and God's favor is given to us because of God's faithfulness to His Word.

Sometimes, when we see God's favor on someone, we become jealous and envious of all their "good fortune" and fail to perceive the seed of favor which someone showed and to which they have become a beneficiary.

In II Corinthians 10:7 Paul tells us that we look at things outwardly instead of inwardly. "If anyone is confident in himself that he is Christ's, let him consider this again within himself, that just as he is Christ's, so also are we." Paul developed a spiritual relationship with Onesimus and called him his brother. Through Paul's acts of charity to Philemon, the walls between Philemon and Onesimus came down. God calls us to seek the unity of brotherhood by breaking down walls which separate that union. A wall is a continuous structure designed to enclose an area, to be the surrounding exterior of a building, to be a partition between rooms, or a fence separating fields.

Walls are erected because of the flesh

Man erects barriers which divide and stop the flow of brotherhood between those belonging to Christ. Life has many walls and fences that divide, separate, and classify. These are not made of wood or stone, they are personal obstructions blocking people from each other and from God. But Christ came as the great wall remover by tearing down the sin partition that separated us from God and blasting the barriers that keep us from each other. Jeremiah 31:28 says, "And it shall come to pass, that like as I have watched over them, to pluck up, and to break down, and to throw down, and to destroy, and to afflict; so will I watch over them, to build, and to plant, saith the Lord."

His death and resurrection opened the way to eternal life to bring all who believe into the family of God. Ephesians 2:14-18 says:

14. For he himself is our peace, who has made the two one and has destroyed the barrier, the dividing wall of hostility,

15. by abolishing in his flesh the law with its commandments and regulations. He purpose was to create in himself one new man out of the two, thus making peace,

16. and in this one body to reconcile both of them to God through the cross, by which he put to death their hostility.

17. He came and preached peace to you who were far away and peace to those who were near.

18. for through him we both have access to the Father by one spirit.

Walls only come down with the Word of God

Paul declared, "There is no distinction between Greek and Jew, circumcised and uncircumcised, barbarian, Scythian, slave and freeman, but Christ is all, and in all," (Colossians 3:11). Without Christ, barriers cannot come down that have been erected. Once Onesimus became a "brother," not only to Paul but to Philemon, the power of the Word could tear down that which was between them.

When Paul asked Philemon to forgive the indebtedness against Onesimus, he was giving an opportunity for Philemon to tear down the wall that was between him and his slave. A debt is something owed which keeps accruing an obligation until it is settled.[1] Jesus asks us to release others by forgiving their debts so that they can be set free from slavery. "For it is for freedom that Christ has set us free. Stand firm, then, and do not let yourselves be burdened again by a yoke of slavery" (Galatians 5:1).

Words and actions are a voice which either enslave us or free us to tear down walls or create walls. In II Samuel 2, we see a fight between Saul's armies and David's. Through a misconduct which ended in bloodshed, Asahel, Joab's brother, was killed by Abner. Joab was going to continue the bloodshed when Abner asks,

26   Must the sword devour forever? Don't you realize that this will end in bitterness? How long before you order your men to stop pursuing their brothers?"

27.   Joab answered, 'As surely as God lives, if you had not spoken, the men would have continued the pursuit of their brothers until morning.'

28.   So Joab blew the trumpet, and all the men came to a halt; they no longer pursued Israel, nor did they fight anymore.

Intercessors become a wall of protection

Blood had been spilt, but someone had to stand as a wall of kindness to stop its pursuit to others who were innocent. A debt had to be cancelled! When Joab blew the trumpet to stop the attack, this act became a kindness to cover the transgression.

Walls act as a barrier between heaven and man

Another example of walls is seen in II Samuel 1. David is lamenting for the death of Saul and Jonathan. He prays that God would stop the blessings coming to the Amalekites. He speaks to the mountains of Gilboa not to have dew or rain. Their fields would not offer their grain for the shield of the mighty (Saul and Jonathan) was defiled. He says the blood of the slain was unsatisfied because they were killed not in battle, but by an Amalekite who did not honor the Lord's anointed. David tells the Amalekite in verse 16, "Your blood be on your own head. Your own mouth testified against you when you said, 'I killed the Lord's anointed.'

Empty vessels become walls for others

There is power within us to be a wall of protection for others or be a wall of destruction by our actions and voice. Jesus came to stop blood guilt and expects us to follow His example. Power to speak against others does not make us great. In the book of James we are told that to be great, we have to be a servant.

Jesus leaves us an example of greatness by emptying Himself of His position as God to become incarnate in Philippians 2:6-8:

> 6. Who, being in very nature God, did not consider equality with God something to be grasped,
> 7. but made himself nothing, taking the very nature of a servant, being made in human likeness.
> 8. And being found in appearance as a man, he humbled himself and became obedient to death—even the death on a cross!

I Peter 2:18-19 says, "Slaves, submit yourselves to your masters with all respect, not only to those who are good and considerate, but also to those who are harsh. For it is commendable if a man bears up under the pain of unjust suffering because he is conscious of God."

Walls of offense

Before Onesimus ran away from his master to find his true Master, his being a slave did not profit him. It was the prayers of Paul that Onesimus was released from one type of slavery to become a slave for the cause of Christ. Why? Because Onesimus allowed God to heal his heart. Whenever there is a wall of offense between us and someone else, our prayers are hindered from ascending as incense to the Father. On the other hand, our anger, jealousy, etc. rise as an incense to draw bloodguilt. The powers to bless and curse are within each of us and we need to know what God wants us to speak.

Hebrews 4:7 says, "Today, if you hear his voice, do not harden your hearts." Onesimus could have hardened his heart when Paul told him to return to Philemon, but he didn't. Something had been imparted into his life that changed him and overrode the memory of being a slave.

The "Good News" is this: we, like Onesimus, were purchased with a price. Evolution didn't change Onesimus anymore than evolution can make us a man out of an ape. Man was redeemed, not evolved!

The connotation of the word "today" is "birthday." The power to suffer for doing right, to be a servant, to be helpful to God and man is in the virtue that comes from the obedience of receiving the word sent to us. It's a new day for us, a day when things change. I Thessalonians 2:13 says:

> 13. When we also thank God continually because, when you received the Word of God, which you heard from us, you accepted it not as the word of men, but as it actually is, the Word of God, which is at work in you who believe.

You see, for the Word to change us, to work in our lives, we have to accept the Word and believe in it to the acting on that Word. It took faith for Onesimus to return to Philemon.

God's Word went into Onesimus to empower him to make right his wrong of running away. His return built a bond of fellowship between him and his master by the act of unity in the faith.

Incense (prayers) ascends when the wall of offense is torn down. Until the wall came down between Philemon and Onesimus, their relationship was in a state of rubble. We build walls within the body of Christ each time we hold on to our methods and motives. It is time we consider others and their part in the kingdom. We need to learn the art of submission to one another as Paul submitted to God's plan for his life.

The wall that is erected after the wall of offense is torn down is the wall of the Holy Spirit to guard and protect us from the enemy. Obadiah 21 tells us that God will raise up leaders to restore God's people as a nation, but the kingdom will be the Lord's. Paul was God's leader to restore Onesimus, but Onesimus was the Lord's, not Paul's slave or Philemon's slave.

Each time we intercede to set people free, we are to release them back to their original owner—Jesus Christ. He bought us with a price. We are owned by Him, not man. When we do not release people back to God, we try to protect from our flesh instead of God's Spirit.

Philemon was being tested in the realm of his affection. God is triune. We are to be holy in our spirits, emotions (affections), and our bodies. Each area will be tested and tried to reveal if there is any iniquity (offense) still hiding.

Paul could have ordered Philemon to forgive Onesimus and to love him, but what test would that be? "But for love's sake Paul appeals to Philemon." Paul demonstrated his love for Philemon and Onesimus by sending Onesimus back to his rightful owner. Paul needed Onesimus and his gift, but he honored Philemon in sending Onesimus home. Paul tells us in verse 15, "Perhaps the reason he was separated from you for a little while was that you might have him back for good."

Unless our heart is circumcised (our ways severed from our rule), we cannot serve God's plans and we will not have the faith needed to possess the promises of God. It takes intercession to bring God's plan to the forefront so that we have an opportunity to choose His ways and quit doing our own ways.

It is not enough to want to serve God; we have to have the power to obey Him. In Joshua 24:22, "The people said to Joshua, 'We will serve the Lord our God and obey him.' Joshua answers 'Then throw away your foreign gods and make covenant with Him.'"

Intercessors tear down foreign gods

A backsliding spirit is a foreign god to which we bow down and serve. Backsliding is our Adamic nature, the old man that has not been circumcised, or born again. It is an iniquity which we must deal with as it keeps us from doing what we want to do for God. Unless we are born again, we can try to serve God from our flesh but without a habitation of God. There are those who want to work for God in doing right things and living by the "golden rule," but what is a rule without the presence of God? We have an example of this in II Kings 10:30-31, (after Jehu oversees the destruction of Jezebel and the Baals):

30. The Lord said to Jehu, 'Because you have done well in accomplishing what is right in my eyes and have done to the house of Ahab all I had in mind to do, your descendants will sit on the throne of Israel to the fourth generation.'

31. Yet Jehu was not careful to keep the law of the Lord, the God of Israel, with all his heart. He did not turn away from the sins of Jeroboam, which he had caused Israel to commit.

Jehu was a type of intercessor who destroyed God's enemies. For this work he received an earthly reward, but not an eternal reward. If we are used in intercession, we leave an inheritance of freedom from certain iniquities for another generation. But if we do not turn away from the sins of our fathers, our succeeding generations after us can get caught up in the same sins that we resisted.

Intercessors ignite others

Intercession not only prepares God's plans for us, but unifies us to God's plans. Intercession is that method to ignite His plans. Ignite means to set on fire, to kindle, and begin to burn. II Timothy 1:6 says, "Stir up the gift within you by the laying on of hands," (fan into flames the gift of God which is in you). Unless there is "ignition," there will not be a performance. Perform means to carry out in action; execute, do, fulfill, discharge as a duty or command, to carry through to completion an action, undertaking, to give an exhibition, display, demonstrate, present or to accomplish. We are to allow the gift (God's plans within) to be ignited. This is done when someone prays for us and virtue is released from them.

Intercessors release spiritual gifts for others

Remember, when Jesus led those in captivity out of captivity, He gave gifts to man. Each time we are taken out of captivity, a gift to serve God is then made available to us so that we can serve God in the very area that we had been taken captive. Without the gift to serve God, we would return to the old nature and return to captivity. This gift that is given to us needs to be kindled, or put into service.

God's gift is the method that He has chosen for us to serve Him. It is His way of doing something according to a definite plan; a mode of procedure; an orderly system. God has the method of intercession He wants us to flow in. Method means a systematic or manner of procedure, an orderly arrangement of parts or steps to accomplish an end. Sometimes it might be praying in tongues, sometimes birthing, sometimes groaning, sometimes laughter, sometimes dance, sometimes whirling around, clapping the hands, jumping up and down, blowing on the person, etc. We are not to dictate the method of deliverance; we are to follow the Holy Spirit who quickens the mortal body. Romans 8:11 says, "And if the Spirit of him who raised Jesus from the dead is living in you, he who raised Christ from the dead will also give life to your mortal bodies through His Spirit, who lives in you."

Intercessors weep and wail

There is an intercession mentioned in Micah 1:8 which most men try to avoid like the plague. Micah says that he will weep and wail, go about barefoot and naked, howl like a jackal, and moan like an owl for the sins of God's people which they have not repented for—because they are left incurable.

Micah says he will also roll in the dust and writhe in pain waiting for relief when disaster comes. He knew that the way was barred until someone came to tear down the wall of hindrance, which is done by intercession. He then says in Micah 4:9 (speaking to the men), "Why do you now cry aloud-have you no king? Has your counselor perished that pain seized you like that of a woman in labor? Writhe in agony, O Daughter of Zion, like a woman in labor."

Intercession is a work, a labor, to restore relationship between God and man. Labor is a process to bring forth the spiritual work of God as a "baby" is brought forth. It is the method God chooses to restore relationships at the appointed time for that relationship to be healed, restored, or repaired. Micah is used to restore the relationships between God and man just as Paul was used between Philemon and Onesimus. Regarding the passage, "O daughter of Zion," daughter means relationship, to build, obtain children, repair, and set surely. God has a "set time" for birthing intercession. In I Samuel 13:8, Samuel set a time in which he would meet Saul in Gilgal. When he didn't show up at that time, Saul forced himself to offer a sacrifice out of fear. For this act of disobedience, he lost his kingdom because he didn't trust God to wait upon Him even if there was a delay.

Intercessors can force labor

A spirit of force can come upon us to bring forth something before its time. If we give ourselves to this force (which is fear), we can lose that which we want to gain.

A good example of acting according to God's time is found in Acts 3. A cripple from birth sits at the Gate Beautiful. Beautiful means hour, season, time. The cripple was at his set time for the miraculous. Peter arrives at a time appointed to speak God's Word. After perceiving that the man had faith to receive, Peter says in verse 6, "Silver and gold I do not have, but what I have I give you. In the name of Jesus Christ of Nazareth, walk."

Intercessors are chosen for particular tasks

Jesus passed by this man many times when He came to the Gate Beautiful, but it was prepared for Peter to do the miracle at the "set time." Knowing that God chooses the intercessor for particular services should eliminate all forms of envy or jealousy against those being used. But this is not the case. Satan begins to speak words to our minds like, "Why wasn't I used?"

Satan knows that which will bring discord to stop intercession.

Without intercession, people and relationships are abandoned or estranged from God by the walls mentioned earlier. Micah 5:3-5 says,

> 3. Therefore Israel will be abandoned until the time when she who is in labor gives birth and the rest of his brothers returns to join the Israelites.
> 4. he will stand, shepherd his flock in the strength of the lord—the sheep will live securely—his greatness shall reach to he ends of the earth
> 5. and he will be their peace.

Intercessors are called great in God's kingdom

Here we have three promises from God. Those who come out of a place of abandonment are able to stand, shepherd his flock, and live securely. It is intercession which causes others to stand, shepherd or watch over their land in the strength of the Lord, so that those under them can live securely. Acts of intercession are spoken of in the spirit world as greatness.

Daughters of Zion (intercessors) are a type of the Ark of Testimony

Intercessors remind the people of their inseparable link between worship and obedience. The Ark carried the articles of the Lord, the manna, the rod that blossomed, the Ten Commandments, and the mercy seat with the statues of angels having their wings stretched out over the Ark as a covering.

The Manna represented God's provision, the Ten Commandments represented God's Word, and the Mercy Seat represented God's nature.

Intercessors must feed upon God's Word as nourishment. They must also obey His Word for instruction, and walk in His mercy as they minister to others.

Mercy, obedience, protection, trust, and the worship of God are taught. We cannot teach others that which we have not learned. If we listen to the teachings of these "Daughters of Zion," we will obtain a garland to grace our heads and a chain to adorn our neck.

Intercessors influence others to act like Christ

Spiritual "daughters of Zion" influence the heart to act in a manner and reflection of Christ. Moses says that the Lord had called him as a nursing mother to carry the children of Israel to be a spiritual influence to us, to nourish us as a mother her child. (Numbers 11:12).

Just as what parents do reflects upon the child, so what we do reflects either for good or bad upon the one who bore us spiritually. John 3:2 says, "I know that thou art a teacher come from God." The ability to teach and train children must come from God. By His Spirit we become a type of the Ark to carry His presence. But what if the "child" we are to carry doesn't want us to carry them?

Not all children listen to their spiritual mothers

In Exodus 4 Moses asks God, "What if they do not believe me or listen to me?" Each teacher experiences the same anxieties that Moses experienced when God told him to go to Egypt and address the leaders of Israel and Pharaoh. "What if our children won't listen to us?" God responds by asking Moses a question in Exodus. 4:2: "What is in your hand?" His answer was, "A staff-rod." "Cast it down."

Cast means to throw down. Unless we lay down in Christ that which is given to us, we will not have the power to hold or pick up and rule as Christ. Casting speaks of change.

The rod spoken of in Moses' hand was for chastising, correcting, ruling, and supporting of life. The Word of God has been given to us as the rod, or staff to rule, support life, and to have power to change ways. The rod is there for us, but we have to pick it up and use it.

When God asked Moses to throw the rod to the ground and it became a serpent, He then said "Pick it up" and it became a rod again. When we pick up intercession, we are given the power to correct or rule in the area of the intercession in His name. Moses asks the next question, "What if they don't listen after they are corrected?" Exodus 4:8-9 says,

8.   Then the Lord said, 'if they do not believe you or pay attention to the first miraculous sign, they may believe the second.
9.   But if they do not believe these two signs or listen to you, take some water from the Nile and pour on the dry ground. The water you take from the river became blood on the ground.'

As spiritual mothers, we are to correct those the Lord gives to us. Those who listen and follow instructions are cleansed or sanctified by the Word. Those who stay in their sins are considered unclean. After a time, those who refuse correction must be released back to God. If we continue to carry them, we become "polluted." Just because we release some back to God does not mean that they are lost. God can raise up another to pray for them and to these they will listen.

Intercessors who nurture others in prayer are spiritual mothers

Nurture means to feed, nourish, support during stages of growth, upbringing, training, and education. The one who nurtures, feeds, and supports during stages of growth and trains in intercession is a spiritual mother. Not every person God gives us will receive the nourishment we give to them. When this happens, the intercessor can become polluted by bitterness.

Intercessors can experience estrangement

One of the things that can happen between the intercessor and the one being prayed for is estrangement or apathy. Another word for apathy is Stoic. According to the American Standard Dictionary, stoic means that which pertains to the philosophy founded by Zeno, who taught that men should be free from passion, unmoved by joy or grief. Becoming stoic is not from God. God is a God of love and passion. He experiences grief when we sin and joy when we repent. We were created in His image to experience these emotions, too. We have to see a future of God's favor for those He gives to us. If we don't, then we have become estranged from God for them.

Character is learned

It is an awesome responsibility to be a mother for others, to seek God's plans for them, and to help them worship and obey Him. Just as we teach our children at each stage they go through, so we go through stages of growth as a mother and must ever be learning and spiritually fed ourselves. Character is learned. We are not to expect our children to just be endowed with godly character. We are to teach by example as well as give them verbal instructions.

Praying for others to tell them about Jesus is a character trait that comes through having intimacy with Jesus. Intimacy involves cycles in relationships:

1. The level of parent to child
2. The level of Christian to Christian
3. The level of parent submitting to the gift in the child.

All of us do not have the same gift, but we are all to be fitly joined together so that we do not lack any of God's gifts. As spiritual parents, we are to expect maturity, growth and leadership. The spiritual parent learns to submit to the gift of the child just as the child submits to the gifts of the parent until "all" reach the desired place God has for us.

Prayer enhances the vision for others

Spiritual mothers represent Jesus as mediators who offer up prayers that enhance the vision God gives. In the book of Joel, God says that the only way to avert the judgment that God sees for His people is for Joel to see the sins of Israel and to repent for them. Joel was told that if he did this, then maybe God would send a blessing instead of judgment on the people.

Judgment creates a vacuum

Earlier I spoke on forensic intercession coming at the time of judgment. Another aspect of intercession is seen at this time because a vacuum is created when judgment is released much like the vacuum created when streaks lightning across the hemisphere. We see this in type in Revelation 8:5 "Then the angel took the censer, filled it with fire from the altar, and hurtled it on the earth; and there came peals of thunder, rumblings, flashes of lightning and an earthquake."

Thunder is heard by the effects of the lightning streaking across the sky which caused a vacuum in the atmosphere. When a vacuum is created in a person's life at the time of judgment, he stands as it were, between two hemispheres—the one being light and the other being darkness. Judgment demands choices. The person being judged will either accept the judgment and repent or hate God all the more and continue in darkness.

When this happens, intercession is released for that person to fill himself with God's presence so that he will not fill himself with Satan's attributes. Man needs something to hold onto. We are like Tarzan swinging through the jungle. If there is not a rope to grab, we will not let go of the rope we are holding. Emptiness is scary!

Jesus emptied Himself

In every aspect of interceding that we will experience, Jesus experienced it first. Philippians 2 gives us a quick glance of the examples we are to see:

6.   Who, being in very nature God, did not consider equality with
       God something to be grasped,
7.   but made himself nothing, taking the very nature of a servant,
       being made in human likeness.
8.   And being found in appearance as a man, he humbled himself
       and became obedient to death—even the death on a cross!'
9.   Therefore God exalted him to he highest place and gave him
       the name that is above every name,
10.   that at the name of Jesus every knee should bow, in heaven
       and on earth and under the earth,
11.   and every tongue confess that Jesus Christ is Lord, to the glory
       of God the Father.

Unless we learn how to be emptied in Christ, the enemy will come with lies to stir up our flesh, thus rendering us useless to intercede for another. Notice, it is Jesus interceding through the vessel who has been emptied in Christ so the intercession can bring glory to the Father. Without the continual emptying, we will be tempted to exalt our work and pride will bring our downfall.

The emptying is releasing persons we have held in our spirits and soul back to God which will happen several times so that the intercessor can be refilled with God's power and kept for Him.

Intercessors experience the fear others are feeling

When we are afraid of judgment, our eyes are not seeing the benefit of correction. Spiritual mothers run the gamut of emotional upheavals and have to be aware of continually washing the soul in the Word of God when they intercede for others. We do not ever want to come to a place in which we hinder our spiritual children from coming to God or receiving directly from His presence.

Intercessors can be rejected

An example of intercessors being rejected is seen in Luke 19:14. "But his subjects hated him and sent a delegation after him to say, 'We don't want this man to be our king.'" Intercessors are those who submit to Jesus to rule over the lives of others in prayer. There are times that the prayer will be in the authority in his kingly office. Intercessors "watch over the souls" of those given to them just as a king is to watch over his subjects. He does this to kept them safe in the kingdom of God. But, just as this king in Luke 19:14 was rejected, intercessors can and are often rejected.

Intercessors can reject their assignments

On the flip side, intercessors can reject or refuse the position to watch over some. Instead, they will hide their gift in themselves and refuse the assignment.

Intercessors have to contend for their faith

In Jude we are urged to contend for the faith that was entrusted to the saints. Godless men creep into our midst to take us away from the truth of God to cause us to leave walking in the spirit to a place of immorality. Intercessors will be judged for any immoral act along with the worst of sinners if they leave their faith in God. Verse six stands as a warning to all intercessor, "And the angels who did not keep their positions of authority but abandoned their own home—these are kept in darkness, bound with everlasting chains for judgment on the great Day."

Intercessors experience joy

Intercession is not always doom and gloom. There are times of exceedingly great joy. Intercessors need to be reminded, though, that they are to count it a joy to pray for others (James 1). Joy gives us the strength to inhabit for rule in intercession; it is a gift for those completing their assignments. Joy involves appreciating the call of God to pray. Joy is manifested when we look into the future for "better things to come" for the person in need.

Intercessors are to please the Father

Being a good spiritual intercessor is all about finding out what pleases the Father. When our ways please the Lord, He will make our enemies our footstool and allow others to see the work of intercession and desire it to the glory of God. Yes, intercession is a sacrifice, but with more rewards attached to it than when we do not pray.

Chapter 4

Prayers Picked Up By Demonic Spirits

What? Do you mean to tell me that I can pray wrong? That Satan can actually get my prayers and not God? We have to know that God has an adversary. His name is Satan. That means we have an adversary. His plan is to stop our prayers from either getting answered or getting answered in such a way that we become discouraged and quit praying. Let's look at the story of Saul as he prays using God's enemies in I Samuel 28:

3. Now Samuel was dead, and all Israel had lamented him, and buried him in Ramah, even in his own city. And Saul had put away those that had familiar spirits, and the wizards, out of the land.

4. And the Philistines gathered all Israel together, and they pitched in Gilboa.

5. And when Saul saw the host of the Philistines, he was afraid, and his heart greatly trembled.

6. And when Saul inquired of the Lord, the Lord answered him, neither by dreams, nor by Urim, nor by prophets.

7. Then said Saul unto his servants, Seek me a woman that hath a familiar spirit that I may go to her, and inquire of her. And his servants said to him, Behold, there is a woman that has a familiar spirit at Endor.

8. And Saul disguised himself, and put on other raiment, and he went, and two men with him, and they came to the woman by night: and he said, 'I pray thee, divine unto me by the familiar spirit, and bring me him up, whom I shall name unto thee.'

9. And the woman said unto him, 'Behold, thou knowest what Saul hath done, how he hath cut off those that have familiar

spirits, and the wizards, out of the land: wherefore then layest thou a snare for my life, to cause me to die?'

10. And Saul sware to her by the Lord, saying, 'As the Lord liveth, there shall no punishment happen to thee for this thing.'

11. Then said the woman, 'Whom shall I bring up unto thee?' And he said, 'Bring me up Samuel.

12. And when the woman saw Samuel, she cried with a loud voice: and the woman spake to Saul, saying, 'Why hast thou deceived me? For thou art Saul.'

13. And the king said unto her, 'Be not afraid: for what sawest thou?' And the woman said unto Saul, I saw gods ascending out of the earth.'

14. And he said unto her, 'What form is he of?' And she said, 'An old man cometh up; and he is covered with a mantle.' And Saul perceived that it was Samuel, and he stooped with his face to the ground, and bowed himself.

15. And Samuel said to Saul, 'Why hast thou disquieted me, to bring me up?' And Saul answered,' I am sore distressed; for the Philistines make war against me, and God is departed from me, and answereth me no more, neither by prophets, nor by dreams: therefore I have called thee, that thou mayest make known unto me what I shall do.'

16. Then said Samuel, 'Wherefore then dost thou ask of me, seeing the Lord is departed from thee, and is become thine enemy?

17. And the Lord hath done to him, as he spake by me: for the Lord hath rent the kingdom out of thine hand, and given it to they neighbor, even to David:

18. Because thou obeyest not the voice of the Lord, nor executedst his fierce wrath upon Amalek, therefore hath the Lord done this thing unto thee this day.'

In the above account, Saul put away witchcraft and sorcery from the land, but not from his heart. When God did not answer him, he looked to the occult (prayer) for a sound to give him instruction.

Satan's prayers rise from the Abyss

As we have said earlier, prayers are equated with incense. In Revelation 8 the smoke of the incense rose up before God. In Revelation 9:2-3, smoke rose from the Abyss which darkened the sun and sky and then came down upon the earth. Out of the smoke came locusts with power to harm those who did not have the seal of God on their foreheads. Satan has people praying to kill and destroy God's people just as God has those who pray to protect and bless God's people. They might be doing this overtly or advertently.

Satan receives prayers

The prayers that are in Christ ascend to the Father. Prayers that stem from envy, jealousy, anger or from evil spirits are received in darkness. Turn to Isaiah 14:9: "The grave below is all astir to meet you at your coming; it rouses the spirits of the departed to greet you—all those who were leaders in the world; it makes them rise from their thrones-all those who were kings over the nations." From II Kings 16 and II Kings 18 we have two examples regarding prayers. First, we'll look at Ahaz, King of Judah:

2. But he did not follow the Lord as his ancestor David had; he was as wicked as the kings of Israel.
3. He even killed his own son by offering him as a burnt sacrifice to the gods, following the heathen customs of the nations around Judah—nations which the Lord destroyed when the people of Israel entered the land.
4. He also sacrificed and burned incense at the shrines on the hills and at the numerous altars in the groves of trees.

King Ahaz's character was evil. He wanted the altar of God to offer up incense only so he could get revelation from God, but offered sacrifices on the heathen altar for himself and his people to appease the foreign ones. Example two: King Hezekiah. It is said of King Hezekiah's character that he was good (similar to that of his ancestor David).

4. He removed the shrines on the hills, broke down the obelisks, knocked down the shameful idols of Asherah, and broke up the bronze serpent that Moses had made, because the people of Israel had begun to worship it by burning incense to it; even though, as King Hezekiah pointed out to them, it was merely a piece of bronze.
5. He trusted very strongly in the Lord God of Israel. In fact, none of the kings before or after him were as close to God as he was.

6. For he followed the Lord in everything and carefully obeyed all of God's commands to Moses.
7. So the Lord was with him and prospered everything he did.

Creation groans

Judgment is not only upon man, but upon that which God created. In Isaiah 14 we see that Satan was cast down to earth because he wanted to ascend above God and sit on His throne. When he was cast down, the earth became affected by his evil and groans until the time of its redemption. Romans 8:22 says, "We know that the whole creation has been groaning as in the pains of childbirth right up to the present time."

Earlier we saw how intercessors can experience groaning when the Holy Spirit speaks through them. Humans are not the only things God uses to intercede as seen in Isaiah 23:1-4 where we read of sea, ships, and land wailing in anguish for the things which are about to come:

1. Wail, O ships of Tarshish! For Tyre is destroyed and left without house or harbor. From the land of Cyrus word has come to them.
2. Be silent, you people of the island and you merchants of Sidon, whom the seafarers have enriched.
4. Be ashamed, O Sidon, and you, O fortress of the sea, for the sea has spoken:

God allows the powers of darkness to judge disobedience

God cannot allow anything that has been touched by evil to stand. All must be purged by fire. If He does not purge the earth completely which He will in the last days, evil will rise again to rebel against God and His plans just as Saul raised up the spirit of Endor. In Isaiah 14:24-26 the Lord Almighty says,

24. Surely, as I have planned, so it will be, and as I have purposed, so it will stand.
25. I will crush the Assyrian in my land; on my mountains I will trample him down, His yoke will be taken from my people, and his burden removed from their shoulders.

26. This is the plan determined for the whole world; this is the hand stretched out over all nations. For the Lord Almighty has purposed, and who can thwart him? His hand is stretched out, and who can turn it back?

Judgments by using wars and nature are in God's plan to judge; But Satan has a plan also, to destroy as seen in Isaiah 10:5-7:

5. Woe to the Assyrian, the rod of my anger, in whose hand is the club of my wrath!"
6. I send him against a godless nation, I dispatch him against a people who anger me, to seize loot and snatch plunder, and to trample them down like mud in the streets.
7. But this is not what he intends, this is not what he has in mind: his purpose is to destroy.

His plans to destroy us vary. He tries to poison our minds with hate, seduce us to immorality, and entice us to abandon our faith in God.

God is jealous to save us

As an act of His jealous love to keep us close to Him, He sent His Son Jesus as a type of "cupbearer" to taste the poisonous words of evil first. Intercessors are a type of "cupbearer" who touch evil in their spirits so that others can be set free. An example of this is seen in the story of Nehemiah the cupbearer to King Artaxerxes. The word *cupbearer* means "cause to drink." In the days of Nehemiah, to ensure that the king would not be poisoned, a cupbearer would taste the food and drink the wine first. Then, if he didn't die, the king would eat the food and drink from the cup. This was probably only part of a cupbearer's duties, but it is the one I want to address.

Intercessors are a type of cupbearers

When intercessors pick up something in the spirit world, it is as if they have tasted it. Sometimes they "feel" as if they have tasted hate, immorality, or even lack of faith. At times what they are feeling for others is hard to differentiate between the assignment and their spirit. An excellent example of dealing with poison is seen in II Kings 4:38-41 where one of the "prophets in training" went into the field to gather vegetables, but picked some wild gourds by accident. The gourds were poisonous. Elisha didn't pour out all of the pot, instead, he instructed meal (a type of the Word of God) be brought and placed into the pot.

What we learn from this is that the Word of God will separate between our soul and the Spirit of intercession. The Word placed inside of our spirit will speak a certain sound to our tormented soul that all will be well.

Intercessors have experienced the merger between good and evil many times and know that only the Word has the power to keep them from abandoning the intercession. The Word of God silences the flesh while strengthening the spirit within so that the work can be completed.

The situation with the poison just mentioned was "accidental poisoning." What this means is, while in intercession, people can speak words to us that hinder the intercession by stirring up our soul. Not all poison is accidental. Satan sends out his spirits to destroy intercession with planned strategy. Regardless, the answer remains the same and that is to use the Word of God to purify and separate. It is futile to attempt to argue with the words of doubt, unbelief, and fear which have entered. Only the Word of God has the power to separate between good and evil.

False intercession

Remember this, Satan is a liar! He will attempt to seduce us into thinking that we need to carry things which we are not to carry. We see many needs—but God has not given us everybody. Any intercession that we take on in our own cognizant will open the door to the enemy in the following ways:

1. It opens the door to pride.
2. It places us in a position to be judged.
3. It leaves us unprotected.
4. It leaves a heritage of evil to attack our children.

We are told in Exodus 20:5 that the punishment for not following God descends as an iniquity to our children and children's children because disobedience invokes God's jealousy. In the commentary from the Quest Bible on Joel 2:18 regarding God's jealousy we read,

God's jealousy is an expression of his deep love for and commitment to his people. It stems from a love that claims a special relationship with the beloved. If a wife turns her attention to another man, the husband, because he cares about her, acts to recover her. God could have wiped his hands of Israel, but instead he used a foreign oppressor to convince his beloved to return.

Intercession taken on by the soul is an act of leaving God's plans to follow our own plans, even in prayer. It sounds good and noble, but not all needs are given to us under "spiritual authority." The difference is this, all may pray, but only those with the authority of the Spirit intercede by the Spirit. All "intercession" must be by His Spirit. God is jealous for us to follow Him in intercession.

Law of Jealousy

There is a "Law of Jealousy" which involves the test for faithfulness or unfaithfulness found in Numbers 5: 11-31. Intercessors will be tested as to their faithfulness to follow God's Spirit. This test involved the drinking of a special cup prepared by the priest. The cup contained holy water and dust from the tabernacle floor. When a woman was suspected of being unfaithful, she was asked, "Have you been unfaithful?" If she said no, then she was to drink the cup. If she has lied and has been unfaithful, a curse comes upon her. Her abdomen would swell and her thigh would waste away. If she was faithful, no curse came to her.

This is the application: we are to be faithful to God's plans. Attempting to intercede in the gifting of "tongues" by our soul is an act of unfaithfulness to God. It is an act of taking glory to our selves and is as the sin of Korah found in Numbers 16. Korah became insolent against spiritual authority, Moses, and desired to take the leadership by himself. He declares that he is just as holy as Moses; therefore he has a right to operate in the power of Moses. His accusations and God's responses are seen in the following.

3. They came as a group to oppose Moses and Aaron and said to them, 'You have gone too far! The whole community is holy, every one of them, and the lord is with them. Why then do you set yourselves above the Lord's assembly?'

4. When Moses heard this, he fell facedown.

5. Then he said to Korah and all his followers: 'In the morning the Lord will show who belongs to him and who is holy, and he will have that person come near him. The man he chooses he will cause to come near him.

6. You, Korah, and all your followers are to do this: Take censers

7. and tomorrow put fire and incense in them before the Lord. The man the Lord chooses will be the one who is holy. You Levites have gone too far!'

18. So each man took his censer, put fire and incense in it, and stood with Moses and Aaron at he entrance to the Tent of Meeting.

19. When Korah had gathered all his followers in opposition to them at the entrance to the Tent of Meeting, the glory of the Lord appeared to the entire assembly.

20. The Lord said to Moses and Aaron,

21. 'Separate yourselves from this assembly so I can put an end to them at once.'

What happened next was this; the fire of God came and destroyed the two-hundred and fifty men who opposed God's assignment upon Moses. God is jealous to keep His intercession pure and to keep us in reverence to Him. He does not want to send fire down on us to kill us when we make a mistake, but He will warn! Also, intercession from our flesh draws demonic attack.

Intercessors can be as unfaithful wives to God

If we either take God's glory or Satan's lies in our hearts, we become unfaithful wives praying from our soul drawing the curse of unfaithfulness to come to us. "This is the Law of Jealousy." There is another type of poison which enters our minds and hearts by listening to those in abusive situations, T.V. and soap operas. If we do not release this poison to Jesus, we become polluted.

Remember, everything in the Old Testament is a teaching tool for us today. The law of jealousy is a graphic reminder of the fact that Jesus bore our sins and drank the cup for us. We are just His expression on earth to draw all to Him. Remember this also, intercessors come under a higher judgment from God than those who do not know the Word.

Acts of unfaithfulness reveal a divided heart. Without a heart after God, we will follow our own dictates and sin against God. Because of the fall of man, the heart of man was corrupted with evil. The only way to have a heart after God was for Jesus to give his life to redeem our carnal hearts. If we truly want His heart, He will give it to us. I will list four attitudes of the heart:

1. The heart of David: This is one who has a heart after God's own heart.
2. A divided heart: A divided heart is one having his own desires, but asks for God's word to be given to him without judging his desires first.
3. The heart of the sorcerer (sorcery). If we are looking to something God has not given to us, then we are looking to another spirit to fill that need, which is the spirit of sorcery. Hosea 4:12 says, "My people consult their wooden idol, and their diviner's wand informs them; for a spirit of harlotry has led them astray, and they have played the harlot, departing from their God."
4. The evil heart: "See to it, brothers, that none of you has a sinful, unbelieving heart that turns away from the Living God" (Hebrews 3:12).

The eating of the Passover meal (which involves drinking from the cup of the new covenant) has power to preserve, protect, safeguard, defend, and celebrate the unity with the Father. It symbolizes God's desire for companionship, friendship, partnership, and covenant with the Lord. The giving of the feast of unleavened bread was to teach us that sin breaks this fellowship with the Father and releases His jealousy to have us return to Him.

Seeking after God is life to us

Amos 5:14 says, "Seek good, not evil, that you may live. Then the Lord God Almighty will be with you, just as you say he is." It is not enough to say that God is with us and take the communion of Christ and then do our own thing. We have to seek Him and obey His desires for our lives.

The word "know" is an intimate word meaning oneness and unity. We will never hear the voice of God if we are not in unity with Him. As we seek God for our lives, others will see our submission to Him. We are not only to be in union with the Father, His Son, and the Holy Spirit, but with those who are of His family.

Intercessors are to dwell in the Lord

God has chosen to build a house in which He would dwell, or take up His abode. It was not to be one made with wood or steel beams, but a house which He formed from the dust of the earth and in which He breathed in eternal life. He would furnish His house and equip it for service, of whose house we are, if we hold fast the confidence and hope in Christ (Hebrews 3:6).

Just as the Father prepares a house for us to dwell with Him, so we must desire to be with Him. By giving us a free will, the Father opened up His heart to be grieved by our refusal of His presence. In order to know the Father, we must open up our hearts to have our iniquities revealed and crucified in Christ Jesus. Any thought or emotion which does not line up with His is to be cast down.

God's eyes search the earth to find those whose heart is truly His. If we truly love Him, we will serve Him with our hearts, and not just with our mouths. Then we will be able to love and serve others from a pure heart. When our heart is right toward God, we will ask God for the way He wants to do things. When our ways do not line up with His ways, we will gladly give up our ways for His.

Intercession must agree with God's plans

God has called us to walk by His side in agreement with His plans. We are to walk in His light. To do this, we must leave all that is darkness. This is where our will comes into action. We choose to either walk in the light or to walk in the darkness of our flesh.

When we do not seek God's face to find out His desires, we are under a spirit of harlotry. Harlotry is setting one's heart on himself. It is a heart that does not want to share his love with God.

Our standing before God does not consist on what we have done, but on our faith in that which Jesus has done for us. Because of this, we owe Jesus everything. There is no reason for our boasting. He brought us into union with the Father and destroyed the powers of darkness over our lives. Jeremiah 3:21-23 says,

21. A cry is heard on the barren heights, the weeping and pleading of the people of Israel, because they have perverted their ways and have forgotten their God.
22. Return, faithless people; I will cure you of backsliding.
23. Yes, we will come to you, for you are the Lord our God.

Satan comes to cause us to backslide

It says in Genesis 3 that the serpent was more crafty than any other beast of the field. He said to the woman, *indeed, has God said*? God created the world and all that is in existence with the word of His mouth. To pervert God's ways, man had to speak out words that Satan induced. James 3:6 says,

"The tongue also is a fire, a world of evil among the parts of the body. It corrupts (poisons), the whole person." To restore the whole body, Jesus had to speak the Word when He confronted Satan. We will have to do the same to walk in deliverance. Turn to John 1: 1-2:

1. In the beginning was the Word, and the Word was with God, and the Word was God.
2. He was in the beginning with God. All things came into being through Him; and apart from Him nothing came into being that has come into being. In Him was life; and the life was the light of men. And the light shines in the darkness; and the darkness did not comprehend it. (N.A.S.)

Satan cannot comprehend truth as he is so full of lies. He actually thought that he could tempt Jesus into sinning with either His mouth or actions then we would have no hope in resisting him.

Spoken words must respond in belief

How many times have we prayed to God in the name of Jesus with our mouths yet with our hearts hold unbelief? This is speaking deceitfully. Knowing God is ultimate for our existence. "So, let us know, (be acquainted with, identify, understand, experience, recognize) Him. Let us press on to know the Lord, His going forth is as certain as the dawn; and He will come to us like the rain, like the spring rain watering the earth" (Hosea 6:3).

God can hear the sound of lip service

There are those who say they love the Lord and want to keep His Word, yet they only give lip service to God. II Chronicles 7:17, 18 says, "If you walk before Me, as David walked, and do according to all that I have commanded you, and if you keep My statutes and My judgments, then I will establish you and your kingdom."

Satan does not want us to give up worshipping our gods. He has an investment in our lives and will seduce people to come against witnessing for God. Paul, while under a religious spirit, thought his actions would please God. But, in reality, he was serving a false god, coming against the true God. Once God revealed the truth to him, Paul gladly gave up the deception and walked in the light.

We cannot serve two masters

Paul tells us in II Corinthians 10:3-5 that we have to choose the one we will serve and fight against the one we reject. He says,

3. For though we live in the world, we do not wage war as the world does.
4. The weapons we fight with have divine power to demolish strongholds.
5. We demolish arguments and every pretension that sets itself up against the knowledge of God, and we take captive every thought to make it obedient to Christ.

Intercessors can become self-seekers

Without allowing the Word to change us by His Spirit, we become self-seeking. Colossians 2:20-23 says,

20. "Since you died with Christ to the basic principles of this world, why, as though you still belonged to it, do you submit to its rules?
21. Do not handle! Do not taste! Do not touch!
22. These have little value in restraining sensual indulgences.

Any action not conceived by the Holy Spirit is sensual in some form and our witness becomes false as stated in I Corinthians 15:15. In order for us to be liberated from that which is false we, like Paul, have to see the truth and come to the light.

Intercessors must love themselves

We have been called to identify with God through Jesus Christ in His life and in His love. There are times in which we seem to feel unloved by God and Satan loses no time in speaking his lies to us that we are not loved. It is at these times the Lord waits to be accosted by us. To accost means to approach. What this means is, will we wallow in deception or run to Him when we feel unloved? This too is a test! Will we approach God with the way we feel? Will our call to Him be because we love Him? We want to be assured by God that He loves us, but do we love Him even in our darkest hours?

Intercessors will be tested

Isaiah 17:7-8 says, "In that day men will look to their Maker and turn their eyes to the Holy One of Israel. They will not look to the altars, the work of their hands." What this means is this: we will be confronted by the things we have given ourselves to instead of being faithful to God. Even if what we have given ourselves to is self-pity, God will send intercessors to intercede for others in this condition, and He will send intercessors to the intercessors when they get caught in this trap.

Intercessors must loosen themselves from traps

When we find ourselves in a trap, we are instructed to rend our hearts from that which caused the trap. Joel 2:12 says, "Even now, declared the Lord, return to me with all of your heart, with fasting and weeping and mourning." Did you notice the instructions given to swallow self-pity? Prayer and fasting.

God's desire for us is to return to Him (in our minds, wills, and emotions) to protect us. He remains faithful even if we are unfaithful. Just as the woman was brought to the priest in Numbers 5 to address unfaithfulness, so we are brought to face our unfaithfulness. Micah 4:11-12 says that we will be brought to face Babylon. Babylon is representative of our idols (adulteries) which we give ourselves to. It will be here that we see what we have made our idols.

Once we repent for our unfaithfulness, God says He will make our hooves like bronze. Hooves like bronze is what will be given to us to destroy the enemy. We will pulverize ungodliness so that we may devote ourselves to being faithful. Unless we can see our idols and destroy them, we will not be able to be faithful to Him. Hypocrisy is when we desire to be faithful to God, yet desire fellowship with the world.

Jesus came to present us to the Father a radiant church. To be radiant means we will be healthy, glowing, joyful, and happy. We will never be happy separated from Him.

Chapter 5

Sounds of War

In the natural, each man has a way in which he responds to threats or danger. These responses are under the carnal nature unless they are redeemed to respond to God's Spirit. James 1:18 says, "He chose to give us birth through the word of truth, that we might be a kind of firstfruits of all created." There is an intercession (prayer) that is birthed into us by the Holy Spirit that will act as war against our enemies with instructions on how to plan the battle strategy desired by God. His strategies birthed into us gives life for others so that a two-fold work will be done:

1. To form Christ in us.
2. To destroy the enemy.

Those who become God's intercessors are enlisted into the army of God, Jesus being the Lord of the Armies. Psalm 110 says,

1. The Lord says to my Lord: 'Sit at my right hand until I make your enemies a footstool for your feet.'
2. The Lord will extend your mighty scepter from Zion, you will rule in the midst of your enemies.
3. Your troops will be willing on your day of battle. Arrayed in holy majesty, from the womb of the dawn you will receive the dew of your youth.
4. The Lord has sworn and will not change his mind: 'You are a priest forever, in the order of Melchizedek.
5. The Lord is at your right hand; he will crush kings on the day of his wrath.
6. He will judge the nations, heaping up the dead and crushing the rulers of the whole earth.

7. He will drink from a brook beside the way; therefore he will lift up his head.

There are two types of people on the earth. They are either centric, those having Jesus in their hearts, or anthropocentric, those who live according to the lusts of the world. These two worlds clash. Effective war strategies are given to those who have Jesus in their hearts.

Knowledge of war can be learned from history

When searching the strategies of great anthropocentric generals who came against every value of true Christians, we see that God has given us a key in which to fight. Attacks come against us individually, collectively, and nationally. By learning about their tactics, we will learn how to defeat the enemies we encounter. Where there is war there is a violation of God's Word. We need to ask the Holy Spirit what was violated and how to repent for the violation and bring restoration to the injured parties.

Intercessors can become passive

One of the attacks of the enemy is to make people passive or aloof. The word passive means to stand away at a distance, indifferent and unsympathetic. When we are attacked or when we see someone attacked, we cannot stand aloof and let the enemy overtake. We are in a war. Carefully consider the following scriptures:

Ephesians 2:13 says, "But now in Christ you who were once far away have been brought near by the blood of Jesus."

II Chronicles 6:40 says, "Now, my God, may your eyes be open and your ears attentive to the prayers offered in this place."

Psalm 130:2, "O Lord, hear my voice. Let your ears be attentive to my cry for mercy."

God harkens to our voice

Another word for attentive is "to harken." Harken means to pick up the ears, cause to hear, give heed, incline, and regard. When we have regard for someone who is speaking, then we will listen to what he says. If I want God to harken to my voices, then I have to listen to His voice and to the voice of those He sends. In Psalm 14:2 we are told that "The Lord looks down from heaven on the sons of men to see if there are any who understand, any who seek God." Doesn't that sound like God "harkens" to our voice?

Harken also means to receive. In John 13:20 we read, "I tell you the truth, whoever accepts anyone I send accepts me; and whoever accepts me accepts the one who sent me." If I listen, give ear to, or regard those God sends to me, then I am listening to God and having regard for Him.

Aggressive intercession

We have to aggressively fight against powers of darkness and wickedness. We do this in intercession and by the command of authority given to us to speak to the mountains and have them removed. For example, we engage in war vocally:

"Satan, I command that evil spirit of being aloof to be loosened from us, for it is written that we have been brought nigh by the blood of Jesus. It is also written that if two agree as touching anything, it shall be granted by my Father. Furthermore, the body of Christ has been given authority to bind and to loose. As I loose us from this evil spirit, I bind us to Christ. It is also written in Deuteronomy 29:29 that once a revelation has been given to me, I have power in the revelation and so does my seed. Luke 10:19 says that I have been given power to trample on serpents and scorpions. I take this power and authority in the name of Jesus Christ of Nazareth to speak to you to leave." "Go, in the name of Jesus!"

There is something very important to remember—God uses our voice to speak, but He is the One sends the message.

Intercession involves worship

After the message is sent, (intercession), we return to God and offer Him our praise and thanksgiving. Without the return to the Lord in praise for what He has just done through us, self will be exalted. Worship God!! Give Him all the glory. Without the return of worship to Him, restoration does not take place. In the story of the ten lepers being healed, one returned to worship Jesus. This person's body was restored.

An example of God binding and loosing is seen in Revelation 9. We are told that one day a great army of 20 million will be released against the people of the earth. This army is like locusts prepared for battle to kill 1/3 of the people, but was instructed not to harm the grass of the earth or any plant or tree. There will be fire, smoke and sulfur coming out of their mouths. The reference to this portion of scripture speaks of revolting, ferocious, and powerful demonic forces. Verse 14 says, "Release the four angels who are bound at the great river Euphrates." God will never be outdone. When the armies of the enemy are released, so will be the angels and intercessors be released to defeat the enemies of God.

War against the works of the hands

We are told that the rest of mankind that were not killed by these plagues still did not repent for the work of their hands; they did not stop worshiping demons, and idols of gold, silver, bronze, stone and wood. There will be a war which will come against the works of our hands that are controlled by self. Now, it's time to look at the two generals who almost conquered the known world, Attila the Hun and Hannibal.

Both Attila the Hun and Hannibal swept across Europe bringing devastation to much of the land and the people like the locust in Revelation 9. We can learn much from these two generals as well as from God's Word.

In any war there are two weapons which must be learned. They are: repentance and the use of God's Word. Without repentance, we cannot stand against the enemy because we remain in our own blood, which is the voice of rebellion. Without the Word sent to us and through us, we speak from our own self and will be defeated.

There is a word called "Yosemite." It has two meanings: one, "the killers are among us," and "Grassy Valley".

Killers are among us

Psalm 23 says, "He makes me to lie down in green pastures . . . He prepares a table before me in the presence of my enemies." The killers are among us, but God is preparing a place for us to dwell, which is in Christ Jesus. This green valley is a place of His Word and of repentance. Without His Word, we have no foundation in which to stand against the enemy. Without repentance our sin draws attacks.

Attila the Hun

Attila was one of the most feared and notorious men who invaded Europe during the 5th century A.D. He claimed to own the sword of Mars. He delighted in war and was prudent, being known as the "Scourge of God." He was barbaric in nature and killed his own brother so that he could reign solely. Attila looked for opportunities to gain land for his people and involved himself in political positions of the Roman Empire. Those he conquered were compelled to serve in his army. He pillaged the churches and slew the monks and virgins. He gained financially by making those he captured pay tribute to him.

Lessons to be learned from Attila

We must claim the sword of the Lord. His Word is like a two-edged sword able to divide asunder. We are to delight ourselves in Him and be prudent, being known as God's soldiers. We are to lift others up instead of ourselves and look for opportunities to help them. We are also to become acquainted with the political arena. Instead of tribute to us, all praise must go to God. We are to tithe and we are to honor our local church.

All of God's enemies must be destroyed. If they are not, they will rise up again to attack. Now, for some personal applications:

Application #1: Bring into captivity the enemies of God. (I Samuel 28:18-19).

> 18. Because you did not obey the Lord or carry out his fierce wrath against the Amalekites, the Lord has done this to you today.
> 19. The Lord will hand over both Israel and you to the Philistines, and tomorrow you and your sons will be with me. The Lord will also hand over the army of Israel to the Philistines."

Because of this disobedience to God, one of his descendants, Haman, attempted to kill all the Jews during the time of Mordecai and Esther.

Application #2. Becoming politically involved (I Peter 2:13-15).

> 13. Submit yourselves for the Lord's sake to every authority instituted among men: whether to the king, as the supreme authority,

^{14.} or to governors, who are sent by him to punish those who do wrong and to commend those who do right.

^{15.} For it is God's will that by doing good you should silence the ignorant talk of foolish men.

If we do not pray for those God has placed over us, we will be in rebellion. Rebellion is a form of witchcraft and our actions will be much like that of Saul who conjured up the spirit of the dead through a sorcerer. This will draw spiritual attacks from the enemy and will keep us from glorifying God in this area.

Application #3. Be faithful to keep your word (II Samuel 9).

David desired to show a kindness to the house of Jonathan, his friend. [He gave his word to Jonathan to be loyal to him and his seed]. After Jonathan's death, David enquired of his descendants so that he could keep his word to Jonathan. Mephibosheth was found. Because David was now king, those of the seed of Saul were afraid for their lives. David, however, said to Mephibosheth, "Fear not: for I will surely show thee kindness for Jonathan thy father's sake, and will restore thee all the land of Saul thy father; and thou shalt eat bread at my table continually."

David's faithfulness to keep his word to Jonathan became the tool for a future deliverance for him. Knowing the meaning of Mephibosheth gives us a clue to God's laws of seed time and harvest.

Mephibosheth's name means: "He scatters shame" or "destroying shame." In the following story David's men were put to shame and thought that David was ashamed of them. But, because David showed kindness to Mephibosheth whose name means to scatter shame, David was delivered from shame. The story goes like this:

David also wanted to show kindness to his friend Hanun, the son of Nahaash, as his father showed kindness to him. In this case, Hanun didn't receive David's kindness. Instead, he responded in an action to cause shame. He took David's servants and shaved off one-half of their beards. When David heard of this, he came out to meet them before they came to him in the city. Thinking to spare them of shame, he sent them to a nearby town to stay until their beards grew back. The men then felt that David was ashamed of them so they hired soldiers to kill those who caused them shame. David sowed into the life of "He scatters shame" and when he needed shame to be scattered, God was faithful to be with him.

David says in Psalm 65:1 that any vow that he performs is performed to God. His kindness to Mephibosheth was not just for the sake of his friend Jonathan, it was to honor and esteem God. Isaiah 53:3 says, "He was despised and rejected by men, a man of sorrows, and familiar with suffering. Like one from whom men hide their faces he was despised, and we esteemed him not." When we do not obey His Word, whether it is not showing respect for our country or honoring our word to a friend, our actions will either justify us or condemn us. They will either show respect and honor of God or disrespect or dishonor to God.

Satan sends out his adversaries to cause shame to God's people. Those who show kindness sow the seed needed to receive the battle strategy to defeat the shame.

Hannibal

The second general, Hannibal, whose name means "Joy of Baal," made sacrifices to gods before he entered the campaign. He not only vowed eternal enmity against his enemies, but had the skill in both cavalry and infantry tactics to war. He knew who to make his allies and how to set ambushes. He used harassments to weaken and wear down the morale of his enemies. He also used deceptive devices to divert attack.

Hannibal was 26 years old when he was unanimously chosen to be leading his people against Rome. We are never too young to be used by God in prayer and to learn battle strategies.

The things we can learn from Hannibal are:

1. We need to be a "Joy to Jehovah" and offer ourselves to Him before we enter any conflict.
2. We need to align ourselves to be against that which God is against and learn many skills for His service.
3. We need discernment and wisdom in righteousness to keep us from presumption.
4. We need to be aware of our words which make our brothers weak.
5. We need to use words of encouragement that build and strengthen.
6. Lastly, we are not to be deceived. We are to know what is going on in our army and the circle of influence around us. We can only lose what we do not give up. If we lay down our lives for the "cause" of Christ, we will not die in vain.

The power to encircle

Hannibal wanted to encircle or compass his enemy so that they would be destroyed. We are to encircle the Body of Christ to protect each other. Compass means direction, to revolve, surround or border. We are encompassed by God's love which surrounds us for protection when we go to war. We are to surround the enemy so that he is kept in check and hindered in his plans to invade.

Unless we let go of everything that makes us strong and secure in the natural, we will not receive the supernatural strength that we need from Him. When we do, we will have power to command, power to be effective, power to change our surroundings, and power to overcome pressure. This power has obligations. It is to be entrusted into the Father's hand.

Power has obligations

II Timothy 1:12 tells us that God is able to keep all that is given to Him. Giving ourselves to the Word of God will keep our garments washed and our minds renewed to the Lord. Attacks come against the strongholds in our minds and souls to make us weak in our spirits. II Corinthians 10:3-5 says,

3. For though we live in the world, we do not wage war as the world does.
4. The weapons we fight with are not the weapons of the world. On the contrary, they have divine power to demolish strongholds.
5. We demolish arguments and every pretension that sets itself up against the knowledge of God, as we take captive every thought to make it obedient to Christ.
6. And we will be ready to punish every act of disobedience, once your obedience is complete.

It would not matter to God if both Attila and Hannibal and countless other armies were to come against us if He has chosen for us to be delivered.

Intercessors can be restrained from war

In Jeremiah 6 God warns the people of Benjamin to flee because He has planned the destruction of the daughter of Zion. (They were not to surround for protection). There are times in which God delivers His people when they are attacked and times in which the attackers seem to triumph. God has to rule and we have to seek Him for His cause.

The enemy's strategy will either be to cause fear to come to our hearts so that we will run when attacked when we should stay, or cause presumption to stay when we are to run for refuge. Thus, the attack is to get us to respond to the attack in our senses and fail to seek God. We need to do the following:

1. We are to offer Him the sacrifice of our "ways." Our best defense is to be loyal to God and to His Word, to be Theocentric. I can not be anthropocentric and Theocentric at the same time. If I am living as the world, then the enemy has permission to destroy me or to render me noneffective.

2. We are to obey God's Word in Isaiah 55:8, to come up higher in our thoughts and ways. We are to know that He will swallow up death and remove the reproaches that are against us (Isaiah 25:8).

3. God always exalts His Word, (Psalm 138). We are to long for His courts (Psalm 84), and glorify the Lord (Isaiah 24:24). Isaiah 46 says that the thoughts and emotions of our spirit are as "Baals" (gods which we have bowed down to against obedience to God). These are the devoted things which we give ourselves to that are not given to us by God.

4. Praise connects us to the covenant of God for deliverance, salvation, and for restoration. We are to enter into His presence and magnify Him (Psalm 15).

5. We need to prepare for war by giving ourselves to God, (Psalm 110). We need to know that Jesus is the Lord of armies and He commands, (Psalm 24).

6. We are to have unfailing love to lead God's people and guide them to the dwelling place that He has for them (Exodus 15:13).

7. We will command the nations and they will come running to us because we have heard from Him first (Isaiah 55:5).

8. We are to put on the whole armor of God, and pray that our leaders will receive the words of God to reveal the mysteries of the Gospel (Ephesians 6:10-10).

9. We are to circumcise our hearts to hear His voice, (Jeremiah 4:6).

10. We are to accept instructions from His mouth and lay up His Words in our hearts (Job 22:22).

11. We are to know that He will deliver us if our hands are clean (Job 22:30).
12. Lastly, we are to be strong in the grace that is in Christ Jesus and learn to please our commander in Chief (II Timothy 2:1-5).

Chapter 6

Establishment

We have looked at prayers established in God and prayers that are established under satanic influences. Now, lets' look at the word "establish" from the Strong's Concordance. The prime root of the word establish is "to rise" in the following applications. to abide, accomplish, be clearer, confirm, continue, decree, make good, help, hold, set up, and to make sure.

Intercession is to establish something for God

In Genesis 9:17 God established the sign of the rainbow as His covenant between Him and all life on earth. In Exodus 6:4 God tells Moses that He had established a covenant with Abraham, Isaac, and Jacob to give them a land of promise. In I Samuel 24:20 Saul tells David that he knew that God had established a covenant with him to raise up Israel. And, in Proverbs 15:22, plans are established by advisors and counselors. Psalm 93 tells us that the world is established and His throne is established. In Acts 9, Paul goes to the priest for letters to take to the synagogue to establish him as the one who has the rights to drag out the believers and bring them to Jerusalem where they could be punished.

We know that the plans established in God will rise up as incense to surround the throne of God and speaks success for His plans as seen in Jeremiah 33:6 "I will bring health and healing to it; I will heal my people and will let them enjoy abundant peace and security." God's ultimate plans are to do just that, bring us to a place of wholeness in Him.

God does the establishing

God releases the power needed to carry out His plans and destroy any enemy coming against His plans. For example, In Psalm 142 David cries out to God for mercy. He says something has come to keep him from succeeding by laying a hidden snare for him. David knew that he had a covenant with God and that as such, God would release any judgment needed to establish him and make him secure.

David declares in verse 4, "Look to my right and see." He does not try to hide anything from God. In fact, he declares that God is his refuge and his portion in the land of the living. He also decrees that the righteous (intercessors) will surround him because of God's goodness. Psalm 7:11-17 says,

11. God is a righteous judge, a God who expresses his wrath every day.
12. If he does not relent, he will sharpen his sword; he will bend and string his bow.
13. He has prepared his deadly weapons; he makes ready his flaming arrows.
14. He who is pregnant with evil and conceives trouble gives birth to disillusionment.
15. He who digs a hole and scoops it out falls into the pit he has made.
16. The trouble he causes recoils on himself; his violence comes down on his own head.
17. I will give thanks to the Lord because of his righteousness and will sing praise to the name of the Lord Most High.

God has to establish our minds

When an evil plan comes and we allow the words of this plan to stay within our minds, then these words erect a foreign god which we then bow down to serve in our minds. God has to destroy all foreign gods. All of the words of unrighteousness have to be exposed and destroyed. Isaiah 44 says that while they exist we will warm ourselves by these fire, which keep us from being established in Jesus.

Attention given to false fires allows intercessors to be surrounded by evil

You might ask, "What does it mean to warm ourselves by these fires?" The answer is to gloat over something. The word gloat helps us identify our actions. Gloat mean to take pride in, revel over, rejoice in someone else's mistakes and one's own rightness. It is an action in which we are not faithful to gird up or protect the person who has either made a mistake or has fallen into a trap of the enemy. It is taking pleasure in someone's hurt.

God has established a covenant with us called an everlasting covenant through His Son, Jesus Christ. He has given us an apportioned land as our sphere of responsibility to present to God as holy. Our responsibility for this land is to establish Him as King of Kings and Lord of Lords in it, which includes our minds, emotions, spirits, finances, and bodies. This is our reasonable service to God.

Intercession prepares our land as the bride prepares for her husband

It says in the Bible that Jesus is coming back for a bride. This bride is to be one without spot or wrinkle. Her home will be in the "City Foursquare," or "New Jerusalem." Jesus promised that He would prepare this city, and prepare the bride to inhabit it. Preparations for this promised place begin with those who have received Jesus as their savior. No man can enter this dwelling place while holding on to that which is an abomination to the Lord. Jesus left us the Holy Spirit to teach us how to govern ourselves after this pattern while living on earth.

Each man's land is to be established upon the foundation of Jesus Christ, who is the Word of God. Any attempt to establish something for God, without having the Word of God, is called manipulation. It is of the spirit of Antichrist. Hebrews 3 says, "We are the house of God, a habitation for the Lord our God to dwell in our midst." Under the law of double reference, there will be two Jerusalems. One will be the place we establish for God individually, and the other will be the eternal city coming down from the Father.

The pattern for establishing our land

Matthew 6 begins, "Our Father which art in heaven, hallowed be thy name. Thy kingdom come. Thy will be done in earth, as it is in heaven."

Without God, anything we establish will be false. Just as Jesus promised to prepare a place for us in heaven, we are to prepare a place for Him on earth. Plans for establishing Him in our land originated in the Father's heart first before seen by us. It passes the heavenlies where spiritual warfare tries to hinder God's plan and keep us from establishing anything for Him. We need to do everything possible to receive these plans by seeking God's face and addressing any sin within our hearts which hinders His plans on earth. The following are promises made to us to encourage us in the building.

Joel 2:32 tells us, "And it will come about that whoever calls on the name of the Lord will be delivered." To these who long for God, He pours out His Spirit to fill their homes with joy. They will act as a calf which has been well-fed and gambols in the open field.

Isaiah 63:16 says, "For Thou art our Father, though Abraham does not know us . . . our Redeemer from of old is Thy name." Each home has to be established in authority. If The Father God is not established, then He will not reign sovereignly over our homes. By the very act of not establishing God as the authority, we have inadvertently asked the Antichrist to rule.

Also in Revelation 21:10, "And He carried me away in the spirit to a great and high mountain, and showed me the holy city, Jerusalem, coming down out of heaven from God." Without a heavenly vision of what God has planned for us, we will not be able to establish God's plan in righteousness. When a vision is given to us, we are to " . . . Record the vision and inscribe it on tablets . . . that the one who reads it may run . . . for the vision is yet for the appointed time . . . though it tarries, wait for it; for it will certainly come, it will not delay" (Habakkuk 2:2).

Unless we receive God's Spirit with the plans to establish, we will not fulfill God's plans. His spirit aids us in standing strong against the forces of evil. Turn to Ephesians 6:10-12:

10. Finally, be strong in the Lord, and in the strength of His might.
11. Put on the full armor of God, that you may be able to stand firm against the schemes of the devil.
12. Your struggle is not against flesh and blood, but against the rulers, against the powers, against the world forces of this darkness, against spiritual forces of wickedness in the heavenly places.

Intercessors must cleanse their land from abominations

This place that we establish on earth is to be free of all abominations. "And nothing unclean and no one who practices abomination and lying, shall ever come into it, but only those whose names are written in the Lamb's book of life" (Revelation 21:27). It is God who gives us the spiritual weapons that we need to drive out the abominations within our vessels. He gave us His Son, who gave His blood and His Spirit to live within us.

On this journey to establish God's kingdom on earth, we confront many obstacles. Each obstacle that we overcome allows us to express more of God's likeness to the world. Revelation 21:5-10 says,

5. And he that sat upon the throne said, Behold, I make all things new.

6. And he said unto me, Write: for these words are true and faithful . . . I am Alpha and Omega, the beginning and the end. I will give unto him that is athirst of the fountain of the water of life freely.

7. He that overcomes shall inherit all things; and I will be his God, and he shall be my son.

8. But the fearful, and unbelieving, and the abominable, and murderers, and whoremongers, and sorcerers, and idolaters, and all liars, shall have their part in the lake which burneth with fire and brimstone: which is the second death.

9. And there came unto me one of the seven angels which had the seven vials full of the seven last plagues, and talked with me, saying, Come hither, I will show thee the bride, the Lamb's wife.

10. And he carried me away in the spirit to a great and high mountain, and showed me that great city, the holy Jerusalem, descending out of heaven from God, having the glory of God:

11. and her light was like unto a stone most precious, even like a jasper stone, clear as crystal; and had a wall great and high, and had twelve gates . . . . and the city lieth foursquare . . .

Notice, this plan includes putting away those things which defile and corrupt which we read in Ezekiel 43:9-11:

9. Now let them put away their whoredom, and the carcasses of their kings, far from me, and I will dwell in the midst of them forever.

10. Show the house to the house of Israel, that they may be ashamed of their iniquities: and let them measure the pattern.

11. And if they be ashamed of all that they have done, show them the form of the house, and the fashion thereof, and the going out thereof, and the coming in thereof, and all the

forms thereof, and all the ordinances thereof, and all the laws thereof . . . that they may keep the whole form thereof.

Established on the Word

God gives His laws and ordinances for His kingdom to us in the Bible, the Word of God. Those wanting to know God will be given understanding of the Word. God's Spirit has been given to us to teach and lead us into all truth.

To get a better understanding of what God wants to say to us, we need to read Hebrews 3:1-6. In these verses, we are told that just as the house of God is holy and He rules His house by laws, so our house is to be holy. We are to hear the laws of God, and then we are to make sure they are carried out in every area God has given for us to rule. This "law of the house" is also found in Ezekiel 43:12 which reads, "This is the law of the house; upon the top of the mountain the whole limit thereof round about shall be most holy."

Once we make a decision in our wills to obey God, then our minds and emotions will follow. Yes, there will be resistance, but God always sends His Spirit to strengthen us against the enemy when we are truly sorry for our sins. We are not to look at the problems, but on Him who is the solution. When we set up the ark of the presence of God in our lives, the enemy will fall. It will be a struggle and warfare will take place. Afterwards, when God takes His rightful place spirit, soul, and body—then the false images will fall.

Life is in the blood

John 10:10 says, " . . . I came that they might have life, and might have it abundantly." The Word says that life is in the blood. Without the blood of Christ, there is no life in the spirit. Cults offer up blood, but not the blood for the remission of sins. The blood they offer up is for Satan to come to the innocent and take them captive. It says in Ezekiel 24, "For her blood is in her midst; she placed it on the bare rock; she did not pour it on the ground to cover it with dust, that it may cause wrath to come up to take vengeance."

Our blood draws demons

The shedding of blood causes the demons to come to the sacrifice to execute wrath on God's children. This is done physically as well as spiritually. Whenever we bite and devour someone by cutting them with insults, we release, as it were, their blood which will attract demonic spirits.

Sin had to be dealt a death blow, but death was not allowed inside the city. Jesus, the Lamb of God, had to go outside the city gates to offer up His blood. Hebrews 13:13 says, " . . . Let us go to Him outside the camp, bearing His reproach." What this means is this: We do not confront demons in God's presence. We will be led by the Holy Spirit to a place prepared for these encounters the same as the Holy Spirit led Jesus into the wilderness. When we come to this place, we will confess our sins and acknowledge Jesus as the sacrifice.

In the midst of judgment there is deliverance

Isaiah 9 speaks about the glory of the Lord coming back to a people who had walked in darkness. It says in the midst of judgment there is deliverance. As soon as we judge the sin or iniquities within our souls we continue to establish God in our midst. There is a counterfeit for repentance. It is called "guilt." Guilt offerings never remove the punishment for sins and cannot bring deliverance. Any sacrifice of guilt allows permission for the demons to come and attack because we have not established the life of Jesus in our midst.

Joel 1:10 gives us an example of what is seen when there is no life. "The field is ruined, the land mourns; for the grain is ruined, the new wine dries up, fresh oil fails." We are a type of land that is spoken of here. This land—our spirit, soul, and body—mourns, lacks fruit, and lacks the anointing of God's Spirit. This is what will happen to all who do not establish God's words in their hearts. Unless a kernel of wheat dies, it abides alone. But if it dies, it will bring forth more fruit. The word that was received from the Father and placed in our hearts must be buried (established) in the sacrifice provided by God. If it is not, then the word will abide alone, which will leave the land wasted.

Life can be consumed

Without the impregnation of the Word with the Spirit, life will be consumed. The letter of the law is death, but the Spirit brings forth life. The Word is under the operation of the letter of the law which is only a school master to bring us to Christ. The letter of the law is under the ordinances of do's and don'ts.

Jesus said, "I have come to give life, and to give it more abundantly." We will never bear the fruit of righteousness apart from the identification of the death, burial, and resurrection of the Lamb of God.

Revelation 5:5-10 speaks about the power of the Lamb slain. The Lamb was able to lay down His life because He knew who He was as the Lion. The death of the Lamb empowers the Lion to take authority over the land, and to rule in the kingdom God has given him. All power and authority is given to us in Christ. Without His sacrifice, there is no power or authority of God. Any other power will be under the operation of the power given by Satan.

When we receive what Jesus did for us in His death, then we can receive what He has given us in His resurrection. Ephesians 2:1 says that we are quickened, we who were dead in trespasses and sin, when Jesus enters our hearts. Quickened means made alive by the Holy Spirit. Unless we have the Holy Spirit's quickening power to be with us and keep us in this process, we will die physically at the hands of the enemy and fail to establish God's plans for us.

Provisions for establishing His kingdom

The Lord never asks us to do anything that He has not already given us the ability to obey. His provision is made through a prophetic word for our deliverance. Not only is a word provided for us with power, but preparations for the burial by the anointing of the Holy Spirit. At the birth of Jesus, God provided men to come and lay their gifts at the feet of baby Jesus. They were gold, myrrh, and frankincense. The gold represented the divine sovereignty of God. The myrrh is mentioned in Exodus 30:23 as one of the ingredients of the "Oil of Holy Ointment," and the frankincense is used for purification and for embalming the dead.

After the Magi gave the gifts to Jesus, Joseph was warned to leave the area and go to Egypt. God provided for this journey by using the Magi's gifts.

This message gives us hope that God will provide for all of our needs also. As He provided for His Son, He will provide for us, His sons and daughters in Christ. We need to believe to receive provision for establishing His land in us. He will not forsake us. He will save us from the spirit of poverty as He saved our soul from death if we believe.

Poverty must be planted in Christ

Those who have been planted in the likeness of His death shall also be in the likeness of His resurrection. We have to "plant" the spirit of poverty, the fear of lack, and the doubts of God's provision for us in Christ. Romans 6:5

tells us how we can qualify to be raised to believe for things. The key here is, "united" with Him.

When we face our fears during times of lack, hardship or death, we receive the power of the resurrection which is the Word that will be given to us to change our situation. The only way we will get this word is if we have followed him outside the camp, so to speak. The very word "resurrection" means arising from the dead. God's power accomplishes this resurrection. I Corinthians 6:14 tells us, "Now God has not only raised the Lord, but will also raise us up through His power." Notice! The power is God. Man cannot raise himself from the dead. It is only by the power of God. Romans 8:11 affirms this, "But if the Spirit of Him who raised Jesus from the dead dwells in you, He who raised Christ Jesus from the dead will also give life to your mortal bodies through His Spirit who indwells you."

Taking our place in Christ

Can you see how important it is for us to take our places in the likeness of the lamb/lion? It is the anointing of the lamb/lion that will bring all the enemies of our Lord to bow or submit to Jesus in us. II Corinthians 10:3-5 commands us to be in readiness to pull down spiritual darkness. That readiness is staying before the Lord. It is one who is established in kingdom principles. Listed below are six scriptural references which apply to the persons established in His kingdom. He will:

1. Trample on serpents and scorpions (Luke 10:19).
2. Move in power using His name (Matthew 28:18).
3. Have signs follow them (Mark 16: 16-18).
4. Speak to the mountains (Mark 11:23).
5. Reveal God's glory to others (Psalm 8).
6. Command the work of God's hands. "Thus says the Lord, the Holy One of Israel, and his Maker: ask me about the things to come concerning my sons, and you shall commit to Me the work of My hands" (Isaiah 45:11).

The law of command is given by God to establish

We can only command that which God has given into our hands. God will never command us to take authority over the enemy while in we are in our flesh. The plan of God is plain. Our flesh can never pull down spiritual attacks. Our flesh must be crucified with the Lamb, and then the word will come forth to speak to the enemy. We are never to presume or assume to confront spiritual darkness with our thoughts or our feelings. Revelation 12:10-12 reads,

> 10. . . . Now the salvation, and the power, and the kingdom of our God, and the authority of His Christ have come, for the accuser of our brethren has been thrown down, who accuses them before our God day and night.
>
> 12. And they overcame him because of the blood of the Lamb, and because of the word of their testimony, and they did not love their life even to the death.

Intercessors must separate themselves

We are to minister to God and for God in His Spirit, not our soul. Yes, we will have positive or negative thoughts and feelings about things, but we are not allowed to have them flow through us when we are ministering for the Lord. We are to be separated. This separation only takes place at the time of death to our souls, not physically. An example of this is found in John 19:33, 34.

> 33. But coming to Jesus, when they saw that He was already dead, they did not break His legs;
>
> 34. but one of the soldiers pierced His side with a spear, and immediately there came out blood and water."

Jesus always goes before us to confront that which we will confront. He overcame so that we can overcome in Him. Jesus confronted Satan at four specific times:

1. Jesus confronted Satan in heaven.
2. Jesus confronted Satan in the wilderness with the Word.
3. Jesus confronted him at the cross for His soul.
4. Jesus confronted Satan in His death in Hell.

We must face each thing the Holy Spirit reveals to us with the vision of victory. Just as Jesus despised the shame of sin and looked beyond what He felt to see the glory, so must we see beyond our sins and iniquities to the hope of being like Him when He confronted Satan. Being like Him means we have His DNA. Or, to put it another way, we have His character and nature. We manifest His life!

I John 1:2 tells us, " . . . and the life was manifested, and we have seen and bear witness and proclaim to you the eternal life, which was with the Father and was manifested to us." The evidence of this manifestation, having the life of the Father, only happens when we pass from death to life with the evidence of divine love for those we used to hate."

The germ cell

His love is the eternal seed which produces His nature. Nothing can reproduce without a germ cell. Just as it takes a sperm from the human father to reproduce after the natural, so it takes the Heavenly Father's DNA to establish eternal life in us. This new life is called the germ cell (spirit reproduction).

It takes the power of the Holy Spirit to bring forth that which we have buried in Christ, so that it might become the incorruptible seed. Turn to I Corinthians 15:

37. when you sow, you do not plant the body that will be, but just a seed, perhaps of wheat or something else.
38. but God gives it a body as he has determined, and to each kind of seed he gives its own body.
39. All flesh is not the same: Men have one kind of flesh, animals have another, birds another and fish another.
40. there are also heavenly bodies and there are earthly bodies; but the splendor of the heavenly bodies is one kind, and the splendor of the earthly bodies is another.

We were sown a corruptible body (having the DNA of our earthly parents). When we sow this body into Christ, it is raised an incorruptible body, (having the DNA of the heavenly). Sowing is a life cycle. We sow continually into Christ the natural ways we respond to evil's desires. When we bring the earthly to Jesus, we are transformed into His character and nature.

Examples of this life cycle are found in John 17:3, "And this is eternal life, that they may know Thee, the only true God, and Jesus Christ whom Thou hast sent. I glorified Thee on the earth, having accomplished the work which Thou hast given Me to do." (Notice the work know). Know means to have intimate relations with, to become one with.

John 17:13 says, " . . . But now I come to Thee; and these things I speak in the world, that they may have My joy made full in themselves." This joy that the Lord is speaking about is the birthing, the bringing forth of the word that came to man as the seed.

Jesus gives His disciples an example of spiritual joy in John 16:21. He says, "Whenever a woman is in travail, she has sorrow, because her hour has come; but when she gives birth to the child, she remembers the anguish no more, for joy that a child has been born into the world."

Spiritual birth comes forth in the presence of the Father after the flesh had confrontation with Satan and overcame. The joy is the evidence that we have brought forth God's DNA in the area that the seed was sown. Remember, the word came as a seed to man; the seed was planted into Christ; the seed was given power to rule over Satan; the seed returns to the Father to be glorified.

Satan does not want to see God's word returning to God. If the word returns to the Father, it will not only bring Him glory, but will reproduce as an inheritance an eternal work for four generations. Satan waits to devour at each stage, but this last one seems more crucial.

The "seed" that is sown as a word is called a germ plasma. Germ plasma is the material basis of heredity (Father's identity). If we are to produce after God's DNA, then we need His Word placed into our hearts. If the word that is sown in our heart is from God, then we will bring forth His Word to a place of manifestation where others can see that His Word produced something.

If, however, we received a word from the devil, then the material basis for the heredity of Satan will come forth. That which we produce will be devilish, evil. Identity means the state of being identical or absolutely the same in character and nature. We will bring forth that which we have received as a seed. If God's life is birthed in me by His Spirit, then I will have joy in my life instead of the torments of the devil.

The child, (the Word given), that comes forth through birthing intercession is symbolic of the life cell of Christ in believers. It also represents the prophetic word given to a person. Words come as seeds into our hearts. The word is but an inspiration of what I can have if it is watered and cultivated. Satan does not want the word of God to manifest in our lives. He knows that if it does, we will have power over him. With this in mind, let us look at Revelation 12:10 . . . "Now the salvation, and the power, and the kingdom of our God and the authority of His Christ have come."

Each word of the Lord that is brought forth from the Father and returned to the Father will accomplish that for which it is sent out. It will produce eternal life. This life will bring His salvation, His power, and His kingdom to us and to our seed.

The Seed destroys Satan' plans

Satan knows that this eternal seed will cast him down. He has to destroy this seed one way or another. His only hope is to cause us to remember our iniquities and hope that we will respond to them. If we do, then the hereditary curses we have been dealing with are passed down to four succeeding generations.

Attacks come against the germ cell to keep it from reproducing the life of God to another generation. This is why a spirit of pride comes at us in four levels. If the life of Christ is destroyed, then the enemy can create his image in our hearts or minds.

All life begins with a cell which reproduces after the genetic makeup of that cell. We have two life cells within us; that of the Eternal Father, and that of the father of lies (Satan). For these cells to reproduce, they have to divide and separate. That which is done in the natural is also done in the spirit. For example, it says in Hebrews 4:12, "For the word of God is living and active and sharper than any two-edged sword, and piercing as far as the division of soul and spirit, of both joints and marrow, and able to judge the thoughts and intentions of the heart." Hereditary curses are the spiritual sins from that those who are passed down from generation to generation.

Evil has to be extracted

Jeremiah 15:19 says, "And if you extract the precious from the worthless, you will become My spokesman." Extract means to pull out. There are things within our hearts (emotions, will, and intellect) which are hereditary factors passed down from generation to generation. There is a time and a season planned by God for this extraction. Jesus said it must be at the time of harvest, when both the good and the bad seeds are gathered together. If you try at another time than the one appointed, the heart will be torn and need repair. This separation will occur in the four areas each man possesses, which are:

1. His spirit, soul, and body.
2. His family and finances.
3. His relationships with others.
4. His church and country.

At the time of the separation, man will experience both life forms and a time of panic and confusion. Remember, during this time our deliverance is at hand **if we turn to the cross**.

Isaiah 22:5 says, "For the Lord God of hosts has a day of panic, subjugation, and confusion in the valley of vision, a breaking down of walls and a crying to (against) the mountain. "The mountain is that which you need to destroy by God's Spirit. God hears the cry of those turning to Him.

God sets before us the blessings and the curses for us to choose who we will establish in our land. We have to choose to go on with God. If we choose the eternal Father, we will render our souls to the cross. If we choose Satan, we will allow our flesh to have its own way. If we yield and give ourselves to the soul, then the cell of our carnal nature will reproduce after the flesh. If we yield to the Holy Spirit, then we will reproduce after the Eternal Father.

We all have the same beginning

Each person starts out as a carnal person. When he asks Jesus into his heart, he becomes a new creation. This new creation is to grow into the likeness of the Father. If he does not increase in God's character, then he will increase after the seed of the old nature. There are those who want to be saved from hell, but do not want to serve and obey Jesus as Lord. They want to keep their old nature.

Jeremiah 10:23 says it is not in man to direct his steps. He will have to either give his heart to God to direct him, or give his heart to the powers of darkness, the god of this world. There are only two kingdoms, two masters. We will either express our love for God by giving Him our hearts, or we will choose to allow the evil to come forth and establish darkness.

Three levels of commitment

The giving of our hearts takes place on three levels. When our heart is given to God in obedience, these levels are: the good, the acceptable, and the perfect will of God. There are also three levels of prayers. In the first level, that which is good, we accept the Word of God for the area we are in. This is the beginning of our journey in learning the character and nature of God. In the second level, the acceptable will of God, we begin to offer up sacrifices (prayers) to God from our soul. Not all prayers are acceptable to God, but we are in innocence.

In this second level of sacrifice (prayers), we begin to know that which is acceptable and that which the Father does not accept. The third level, the perfect will of God, is the prophetic prayer of God upon our lives. It is the crown of His glory by praying His will. At each of these three levels, the enemy comes to pervert that which we offer up so that the sacrifice can be stolen.

Familiar spirits

Each time that we begin to establish something from God in our hearts, Satan sends out familiar spirits to hinder us. He stirs up the iniquities within our souls that correspond to the change we are seeking. Familiar spirits are genetic. That's why we're stirred to do what is familiar—what our parents or ancestors did. These spirits attempt to cause us to react according to our old nature instead of God's ways. God is looking for a people who will freely give themselves to Him during this time. It says in Psalm 110:3, "In the day that the people freely give themselves to the power of God, from the womb of the dawn, shall come forth a new order of priest, that of Melchizedek."

We are to be the new order of people

The womb of the dawn is speaking about Jesus. Just as Mary, the mother of Jesus, gave her womb to receive the eternal Christ, so we are asked to give our spiritual wombs to receive the eternal "seed" when our lower nature is stirred. It says that Jesus came after the order of Melchizedek. Melchizedek was without natural father or mother. He came forth from the loins of the Heavenly Father. When we give our "spiritual wombs" to receive "spiritual seed," we will bring forth spiritual fruit. This seed will not have an earthly mother or father. It will have the nature of God.

False return

Jeremiah 11 speaks about a people who turn back to the iniquities of their ancestors as those who serve other gods. To these He asks . . . "What right has My beloved in My house when she has done many vile deeds? Can the sacrificial flesh take away from you your disaster, so that you can rejoice?" The turning back to our fathers' iniquities is lewd in the Father's eyes.

If we love our own life (that of our father's heredity) more than dying to it at this time, then the power to rule is still in "our" hands and is evidence against us that we are not dead to our flesh. Revelation 12:11 gives us the three signs of overcoming power:

1. The blood of Christ.
2. The word of our testament.
3. Loving not our life unto the death.

When our souls' desires to sin are dead (Romans 7:1), we are free to join our hearts completely to God. Then we will fulfill the purpose for which we have been placed on the earth, which is to establish His kingdom.

Sounds of suspicion

An "uncertain sound" is praying while under a spirit of suspicion. Suspicion is the act of suspecting something without proof. It is looking at something secretly and is under the operation of the demonic world. It is attempting to look into the spirit world while in the carnal world. All it will draw is the demonic. The spirit world belongs to God until He releases it by His Spirit. When He does, then He gives us the power to deal with the knowledge we are given. (Then we can sound our trumpets in prayer).

We must understand that our ways are sinful by nature. Jesus tells us to come up higher, having His nature. We can only come up to His nature to the degree that we cause our lower nature to be crucified in Him. Isaiah 42:1-13 lists promises to those who obey God:

1. They shall be His servants, His elect in whom He delights.
2. He will put His Spirit upon them to bring forth judgments. These will know the love of God and the power of God to keep them.
3. He will arouse His zeal like a man of war. He will utter a shout, "Yes;"
4. He will raise a war cry.
5. He will prevail against His enemies.

Joel 2 tells us to sound the alarm on God's holy hill so that those who hear this sound will tremble. David was told to listen to the sound coming from the mulberry trees to know when it was time for him to go to war. At the return of Jesus, there will be the sound of the trumpet. Sounds have a way of vibrating and traveling through space and time.

The enemy knows if we are sounding God's Word through faith in His Word or if we are as sounding brass. The sounds that come through us by the Spirit of God have the power to open brazen gates in heaven for the blessings of God to enter.

Gates are essential for one to enter and exit the city. The gates have bars across them to enforce the owner's decision of whether to open or close its entrance. These bars are a type of the Holy Spirit. It says in Matthew 18:18, "Truly I say to you, whatever you shall bind on earth shall have been bound in heaven; and whatever you loose on earth, shall have been loosed in heaven."

False prophecies bind

According to Deuteronomy 13:1-5, we are to judge the word given by persons.

1. If a prophet, or one who foretells by dreams, appears among you and announces to you a miraculous sign or wonder,

2. and if the sign or wonder of which he has spoken takes place, and he says, 'Let us follow other gods' (gods you have not known)' and let us worship them,

3. you must not listen to the words of that prophet or dreamer. The Lord your God is testing you to find out whether you love him with all your heart and with all your soul.

4. It is the Lord your God you must follow, and him you must revere. Keep his commands and obey him; serve him and hold fast to him.

5. That prophet or dreamer must be put to death, because he preached rebellion against the Lord your God, who brought you out of Egypt and redeemed you from the land of slavery; he has tried to turn you from the way the Lord your God commanded you to follow. You must purge the evil from among you.

If false prophetic words are given and we believe them, then we can become unestablished in truth. False words need to be destroyed! Let's look at Mark 11:

20. In the morning, as they went along, they saw the fig tree withered from the roots.

21. Peter remembered and said to Jesus, 'Rabbi, look! The fig tree you cursed has withered!'

22. 'Have faith in God,' Jesus answered.

23. I tell you the truth, if anyone says to this mountain, 'go, throw yourself into the sea,' and does not doubt in his heart

but believes that what he says will happen, it will be done
for him.

24. Therefore I tell you, whatever you ask for in prayer, believe
that you have received it, and it will be yours.

25. And when you stand praying, if you hold anything against
anyone, forgive him, so that your Father in heaven may forgive
you your sins."

Hindrances from establishing God's Word

A poor self-image keeps one from taking hold of the promises of God
and speaking His Word. A poor self-image will hinder our prayers and hinder
speaking against that which is false. That is why we must deal with these
false images. Failure to destroy these images allows them to be erected as the
abomination of desolation spoken of in the book of Daniel 11:31-32:

31. His armed forces will rise up to desecrate the temple fortress
and will abolish the daily sacrifice. Then they will set up the
abomination that causes desolation.

32. With flattery he will corrupt those who have violated the covenant,
but the people who know their God will firmly resist him.

It is very important that we resist speaking any sound that can be used
against us such as murmuring or complaining. It is written in I Corinthians
10:10, "And do not grumble, as some of them did—and were killed by the
destroying angel."

Grumbling about ourselves is just as bad as murmuring about someone
else. God doesn't like it! Jesus tells us that we are the righteousness of God in
Christ Jesus. We are the beloved of the Lord. When we do not see ourselves
through His eyes, we look through the eyes of the flesh which always reflects
false images. We follow that which is false when we reject truth. Everything
which is false will be destroyed.

A poor self image is a beast in our land

Revelation 12:11-17 speaks about a beast who is allowed to perform
miracles. Through deception he commands our minds and hearts to erect a
statue (an image) in the likeness of the beast. God says that we were created
in His likeness and His image. The mind and the heart have the ability to see

images. If we obey the Word of God, then we have an image of God. This is why Satan wants other images erected within us. He knows that words create these images. Satan has to use people to speak false words to us in order to take us from God. These wrong images have to be destroyed, not just ignored, by speaking their destruction.

We are to enforce God's Words

Each time we speak God's Word we enforce God's plan for our lives. Jeremiah 29:11-14 says:

> 11. For I know the plans I have for you, says the Lord, plans for welfare and not for evil, to give you a future and a hope
> 12. then you will call upon me and come and pray to Me, and I will hear you.
> 13. You will seek Me and find Me, when you seek Me with all your heart.
> 14. I will be found of you, says the Lord, and I will restore your fortunes and gather you from afar, and bring you back.

We need to expect to see God's plans. Expect means: by reason of thinking, looking for a return or an attitude other than what came against us. We must keep our eyes on the "Likeness of God," and not on the soul of man. David tells us in Psalm 84:4-5,

> 4. "Blessed are those who dwell in Thy house; they are ever praising you.
> 5. Blessed are those whose strength is in you, who have set their hearts on pilgrimage."

Finding God's plan for our lives requires us to take a pilgrimage with the Holy Spirit who will take us to God's Word. When we do not have faith in the word God sends, we will despise what He has given and begin to murmur against others who are speaking the same word which God had given to us.

Disobedience weakens the heart

The plague comes against all disobedience. A heart hardened cannot destroy the enemy, so, it will compromise with the word. Compromise is learning the ways of trickery, which is acting deceitfully. These attachments will come upon our children. Psalm 106 says demons smell the blood of innocence and come to use our children as his sacrifice by making them unclean.

There will always be a confrontation with the devil for each word God has given for us to stand on. This confrontation will reveal areas of obedience. It will also reveal areas where we have compromised with the word given. Areas of obedience will declare glory to God as seen in Psalm 19:1-3:

1. The heavens declare the glory of God; and the firmament showeth his handiwork.
2. Day unto day uttereth speech, and night unto night showeth knowledge.
3. There is no speech nor language where their voice in not heard.

Obedience acts as a "voice" for Satan to hear

"In the same way, you wives, be submissive to your own husbands so that even if any of them are disobedient to the word, they may be won without a word by the behavior of their wives" (I Peter 3:1). "Like Sarah, who obeyed Abraham and called him her master. You are her daughters if you do what is right and do not give way to fear" (I Peter 3:6).

Our behavior is a voice. We can obey a command, but have a bad attitude. Sarah's behavior was with a quiet and submissive attitude which created a voice to be heard centuries later. If our attitudes, actions, and character are not in Christ, then where is the voice which speaks or declares God to Satan? We must get this into our spirits. We confront the enemy to declare God in our lives. Submission to the word of God opens up the heavens for the voice of the Father to be heard. Then, with that word we confront the devil.

We must understand this principle. The declaring of God is not from head knowledge or from a religious spirit. It is through the intimacy of knowing God. The evidence is in the victory we have had over the strongholds in our flesh.

If we are faithful to bring down the strongholds in our minds, which are enemies to the Lord, then we will have a revelation of who God is in our spirit. With this revelation of God, we can speak His Word assured that the victory is ours.

Two types of fear

When we first decide to serve God in the word that is sent to us, we experience two types of fear. One is the spirit of fear found in Isaiah 11:2 which is giving respect and honor to God; the other is serving Him in fear that if we don't obey Him, we will be destroyed. We have already shown the first type of fear, or respect, in the story of Sarah obeying Abraham. The second type of fear is mentioned in Judges 4, and in Joshua 9. There will be a time appointed by the Father when we will confront this fear.

In Judges 4, Barak was afraid of going against Israel's enemy, Sisera. Deborah prophesied that because he refused to go to war without her, the honor of defeating the enemy would be given to another.

In Joshua 9 we read that a tribe of Gibeonites became afraid of being destroyed because God had instructed Joshua to drive out all the inhabitants in the land. In their fear of being destroyed, they devised a plan to deceive Joshua and enter into a covenant with him and his people. Isn't that like most of us? We say we love God, but serve Him in fear of going to hell or fear of being punished. God wants us to know Him intimately, to obey Him out of choice because of love. He allows these two types of fears to grow together for a season, then, much like the parable of the wheat and the tares, He sends the sword to destroy the fears in our flesh.

God sends intercessors to confront fear

Malachi 3:1-5 says that God will send His messenger to prepare the way before Christ. He is a messenger of the covenant, who is like a refiner's fire, to purify those who stand in intercession before God. Fear is contaminating. It will destroy not only the intercessor but the ones experiencing fear. After the intercessor addresses fear for himself, he is ready to stand for others experiencing fear. The one who stands before God will be given God's Spirit to destroy fear much like Jael drove the tent peg into Sisera's head in Judges 4.

Intercession is a type of tasting the "New Wine"

It is written that anyone who has tasted of the new wine (resurrection power) will not shortly go back to the old. We need to eat of our redemptive life and enjoy the newness bought by our Lord. If we do not enter into the joy, we will be tempted to quit interceding.

We have been instructed to taste and see that the Lord is good (to take communion with our Lord by entering into our covenant). A covenant is far-reaching. It is able to save to the uttermost those separated either by physical distance or by sin itself. God said His arm is not shortened that it cannot save those who come to Him.

The return of the prodigal

In Luke 15, we read about one son who left his place with his father and joined himself to darkness. The father never left off praying for the son. One day, the son comes to his senses and returns to his father. Of course, this is a parable of all who have left our communion with the Lord and made darkness our home. Prayers have been made for the son's return. Now it is time to see the son return and have him restored to his rightful place.

To better understand our covenant of restoration and what we can have restored, we need to know what redemption means. Redemption means to ransom. It is to restore that which was stolen by a price. Jesus paid the ransom for the prodigals with the purchase of His blood. It says in Hebrews 9:12 " . . . He entered the holy place once for all, having obtained eternal redemption." Everything that Jesus accomplished for us at the cross is made available for restoration, even if we left voluntarily.

Isaiah 53 gives us a list of the privileges available to those in His presence. While living as prodigals, we lost these rights, but now it is time for all of them to be restored as we begin to see ourselves as His sons and daughters. We have a right to be healed, as He bore our sicknesses. We have a right to be prosperous, as He became poor for us. We have a right to be delivered from sins and iniquities, as He took our sins and iniquities upon Himself. We have a right to have all shame removed. The Lord spoke through the prophet in Isaiah 29: 22-24:

22. Therefore thus says the Lord, who redeemed Abraham, concerning the house of Jacob, Jacob shall not be ashamed, nor shall his face now turn pale;

23. but when he sees his children, the work of My hands, in his midst, they will sanctify My name; indeed, they will sanctify the Holy One of Jacob, and will stand in awe of the God of Israel.

24. And those who err in mind will know the truth, and those who criticize will accept instruction.

Rest for those who returned home

Jesus said that the last days before His return would be like in the days of Noah. If this is the case, and it is, we need to look at the covenant God made with Noah to see what is there for us today. The name Noah means rest. It is said that Lamech, father of Noah, foresaw that God would use Noah to reverse the curse of the Edenic people.

In Ezekiel 14:14 God spoke concerning Noah that he was a righteous man. It says in Genesis 6:22, "Thus Noah did; according to all that God commanded him, so he did." God expected two things of Noah, faith and obedience. Hebrews 11 says, that "By faith Noah being divinely warned of things not yet seen, moved with godly fear, and prepared an ark which would house his entire household while the rest of the world came under condemnation." This act of faith pleased God. It further says, "God rewards those who diligently seek Him."

God is looking for someone in the earth who will stand for his family and others to be brought under the ark of safety. This person is one who receives the prophetic word for himself first and prepares his heart and mind to be able to deliver that word to others in prayer.

The heart needs to be circumcised

Another word for cut is circumcise. It says in Jeremiah 4:4, "Circumcise yourselves to the Lord and remove the foreskin of your heart." Jeremiah 6:10 says, "To whom shall I speak and give warning, that they may hear?" In order for the "prodigal" son to return, something had to happen to his heart. Unless our hearts and ears are circumcised from the flesh, they will not hear God by His Spirit. Without the cutting away of the things we have been listening and tied to emotionally, we will not seek God from a pure heart. Let's see what Ezekiel 11 has to say:

16. Therefore say: This is what the Sovereign Lord says: Although I sent them far away among the nations and scattered them among the countries, yet for a little while I have been a sanctuary for them in the countries where they have gone.

17. Therefore say: This is what the Sovereign Lord says: I will gather you from the nations and bring you back from the countries where you have been scattered, and I will give you back the land of Israel again.

18. They will return to it and remove all its vile images and detestable idols.

19. I will give them an undivided heart and put a new spirit in them; I will remove from their heart of stone and give them a heart of flesh.

20. They will follow my decrees and be careful to keep my laws. They will be my people, and I will be their God.

When Jesus spoke of the parable of the prodigal son, He was speaking of the children of Abraham and his seed. ("Understand, then, that those who believe are children of Abraham" Galatians 3:7).

Our covenant of redemption is in the goodness of God. To those who are seeking His face and looking unto Him, they shall see what the prophets saw concerning those God is calling back to Himself so that they will not be as the son who resented the prodigal's return.

Jeremiah 4:20-22 says that those who will be devastated have no understanding of God. It takes faith to believe that you can ask God to give us a new heart and to bring us back from the places we have been estranged from God. We have to desire the prodigal son's return.

When the Holy Spirit came upon Mary telling her that she would conceive and bring forth the promised child, the Lord Jesus, she believed that there would be a performance of that which was promised. Performance means completion, verification. Each time we stand to pray for the prodigals, we position ourselves to cover them during this journey home. We must believe that there will be redemption for them through our prayers of faith.

Just as there is a time in the natural realm for the bringing forth of a child, so there are times and seasons in the spiritual realm. Each time we pray, there is a season of time allotted for that to come forth. We must not get discouraged if our prayers are not answered immediately; only believe that they will come. They might be hindered, but they are waiting before the throne of God until all hindrances are removed. There have been hindrances to seeing the prodigals return.

Waiting on the promises can be most difficult when the wait is long. But God has given us hope even here in Hebrews 11. He tells us of those who waited even unto the time of their earthly departure, not seeing the promise except "far off."

We must believe that there will be a massive return of God's children back to Him. We must wait in faith. Waiting is a response of faith that God has heard our voice and has answered even though we do not see the answer at this present time.

Waiting is also a type of intercession

The definition for waiting from the Hebrew has the root word to bind together as by twisting; to expect something, look patiently for, and to tarry. In Psalm 25:3, we are told that those who wait upon the Lord will not be put to shame because their hope is in God to answer them. Waiting on God is hope in action speaking as a voice of that which is to come. Our waiting is on the promises He has made. In the writings of Paul, he addresses the waiting, saying that God has not failed to fulfill His promises (Romans 9:6).

God has been making great and wonderful promises to the church as well as to the Jews, yet many of these promises seem to be unfulfilled. God has a set time for each promise He has given. Sometimes the "set" time is missed by delay; other times it is missed by being premature. Our hope is to be in His time and not in our anxieties.

Jeremiah 28 speaks of a people not wanting to wait for the promises of God to be fulfilled in the time appointed. They had been in bondage for a long time and were ready for a "good" word to be given to them. Hananiah (a false prophet) was just such a man to carry the word they wanted to hear. He promised the people that God would break the yoke of bondage from off their necks and release them from slavery in two years.

Hananiah's name means: to implore, to move to favor, be gracious, have pity upon, make supplication, mighty, (god) power, and strong. Hananiah had good traits of God, but even the good that we do or have in us has to be crucified in Christ, else they will be used by the enemy against God. Such is what happened in the following:

12. Soon after Hananiah's message the Lord gives a message to Jeremiah:

13. 'Go and tell Hananiah that the Lord says, You have broken a wooden yoke but these people have yokes of iron on their necks.

14. The Lord, the God of Israel, says: I have put a yoke of iron on the necks of all these nations, forcing them into slavery to Nebuchadnezzar, king of Babylon. And nothing will change this decree, for I have even given him all your flocks and herds.'

God called Hananiah a false prophet because even though God would deliver His people from Babylon some day—at an appointed time—the time was not then. Hananiah was causing the people to act when it was time to wait. Waiting for God's time would have acted as strength to obtain the promises of God. When the people refused to wait, their hearts were being turned away from God. God said Hananiah was teaching rebellion! When God says "wait" and we don't wait, then we are in rebellion. If we wait, then our obedience rises as the prophetic voice.

Words out of season are false words

We can learn the following lesson: A word, even if true when given out of season will not rise to God until the appointed time. That word will be picked up by seducing spirits to be aborted. In the ministry of intercession, the prayers and words which we speak are to be empowered by the Holy Spirit. When they are empowered by our lower nature they are considered false words. James 4:3 says, "And even when you do ask you don't get it because your whole aim is wrong—you want only what will give you pleasure."

Disappointments hinder waiting in faith

Another hindrance against waiting on God is disappointments. Disappointments cause us to focus on failures of others or ourselves instead of on our covenant with God. Revelation 5 speaks about such disappointment. John the Revelator is on the Isle of Patmos and sees a scroll in the right hand of the one who sits on the throne. When he heard that no one was worthy to open the scroll he wept with disappointment. One of the elders said to him, "Stop crying, for look! The Lion of the tribe of Judah, the Root of David, has conquered, and proved himself worthy to open the scroll and to break its seven seals."

Just as the Lamb took the scroll, the twenty-four elders fell down before the Lamb and began to sing a new song. The song they sang was, "You are worthy to take the scroll and break its seals and open it, for you were slain, and your blood has bought people from every nation as gifts for God."

If anyone had a right to be disappointed, it would be John. He was an eyewitness to the suffering and death of Christ. He was there when his fellow disciples were killed. And, he was isolated on an island. Yet, he waited on the promises of God because he knew the Lamb of God, Jesus. While he waited on God, he continued to pray for those being persecuted by Rome.

This is good advice for us. If we are still waiting on something specific from God, let us focus our attention of praying for others. Let our prayers be seeds of faith that God will raise up someone else to pray for us.

Disappointment in man

It is possible to not only be disappointed when our prayers are not answered, but become disappointed when we look at the lives of others who seem to be bogged down in sin. The seeing others in sin is not the only cause of disappointment; it is seeing them stay in a place when God has held out His hand to remove them to a better place. When this happens, we begin to doubt whether our prayers are doing any good. Yes, our prayers are effectual. We have to believe that they are active and instrumental in the lives of others even if we do not see the results we are praying for.

Slave mentality hinders intercession

When the Israelites lived in Egypt, they had slave mentality. They thought that they were waiting on God for four hundred years, but when the deliverer came, they were ready to abandon Him when things didn't go right at the first. When we "wait" on God, we wait with expectation. Just rescuing the Israelites physically from Egypt did not change their mentality towards waiting. Their thinking had to be transformed to know God. To do this, God had to bring them back to their old ways of thinking and judge it according to the Law so that they could be set free in the spirit. Prayers are to be fresh manna, not old, stale bread.

We are told that Jesus came to set us free. Freedom has to be learned by knowing what law was violated. In Romans 5, we read that even though sin entered the world through Adam, sin was not punished by death because the law was not given until Moses. Under slave mentality we do not learn the laws of God, only the laws the flesh demands that we obey.

When circumstances arise to hinder us, we come under the power of disappointment and are held captive until we learn that disappointments keep us from the resurrection power of God functioning in our lives. We have to learn our covenant and the rights that are granted to us through Jesus Christ, our husband in the Church of God.

The Israelites, while in Egypt, lived in dread each day while waiting for a deliverer to come and save them. Paul, on the other hand, learned the lesson of waiting on God in freedom. Philippians 1:20-22 reads,

20. For I live in eager expectation and hope that I will never do anything to cause me to be ashamed of myself but that I will always be ready to speak out boldly

21. for Christ while I am going through all these trials here, just as I have in the past; and that I will always be an honor to Christ, whether I live or whether I must die.

22. For to me, living means opportunities for Christ, and dying well, that's better yet! But if living will give me more opportunities to win people to Christ, then I really don't know which is better, to live or die!

The Apostle Paul knew Jesus and the plans He has for His church. He did not hold this knowledge to himself, but preached the Good News so that others could have hope in a life after death and a hope to live while yet in this world's system.

Acts 8 reveals another case scenario of not waiting on God. Simon the Sorcerer saw Peter ministering by the power of the Holy Spirit and wanted this power for himself. He didn't want to take the time to know God, he just wanted the power "now" so that the power would give him recognition. Verse 20 says, "But Peter replied, 'Your money perish with you for thinking God's gift can be bought! . . . for I can see that there is jealousy and sin in your heart.'"

Continual hurts hinder our waiting on God

God is not distant and uninvolved with us; He cares intensely about His relationship. If he were indifferent about our sin, for example, His apathy would show He didn't care about us as his people. We can come to a place in which we have been so wounded or hurt that all hope for waiting ceases.

When God speaks to us, He always confirms His Word so that we know that it is He who has spoken and not our vain imaginations. During Christmas of 2004, Chuck Pierce from "Pray for America" came to Fresno to speak as God's prophet. He said the Body of Christ has been deeply hurt in their emotions due to disappointments of not seeing answers to their prayers. They have come to a place that they become afraid of believing for things or of believing that God will heal those they pray for. (These stop waiting on the Lord). He said he saw a shaking which knocked off all the lights and ornaments on the Christmas tree. He was told that God had to remove the ornaments in order to realign them in order.

The reason for this was that we need to see things through the eyes of God. If we do not turn to God to heal us and fill us with His joy, we will turn to delusion and our eyes will see things that are false. Delusion means: a false belief or opinion; resistant to reason with regard to actual things or matter or fact; dominating, or persistent mental conception.

When we hold hurts within our emotions, Satan comes with false words to take us away from reason. He reinforces our false opinions by dominating spirits until we are so weak spiritually that the ability to wait on God is taken from us. We have to believe and confess the Word and choose to look at emotional scars within and make an exchange of joy to replace the hurts. Calvary is the place of exchange. Without our repentance for holding on to the hurts, we miss Calvary and miss the life God has for us. Quoting from Mr. Pierce:

> Life," he says, "is the property in humans that makes it possible for them to obtain supply which will produce energy, create growth, adapt themselves to their surroundings and reproduce their kind. It also means to possess vitality; to have life active and vigorous; to be devoted to God; to be blessed; to be among the living (not lifeless), to enjoy real life, to be fresh, strong, efficient, active, powerful; endless in the kingdom of God.

In Chuck Pierce's book he addresses the next place in God's destiny for us. He said God would take us to a place so that our "old grave clothes" could be removed. In this place we were to expect instructions and revelation. Psalm 3:4 says, "He answers me from His holy hill." From the Lord comes deliverance (Psalm 3:8). We can choose things to gratify us, but these things become self-seeking and will have no real value in changing us if God's Word is not imposed. It takes the Word and the seeing by God's Spirit to change or transform us from death to life.

Flattery keeps us from waiting on God

Isaiah 6:9 says that there are those who see, but don't see, and if they could see, God would heal them. God was speaking about revelation knowledge to open our eyes to our iniquities. The enemy doesn't want our eyes to see, as seeing will bring forth healing. He uses distractions and, according to Job 17:5, flattery, which causes our eyes to fail.

John 9:11 says, "The man they call Jesus made some mud and put it on my eyes. He told me to go to Siloam and wash. So I went and washed, and then I could see." Jesus had to show the blind man that while we are in the earthly state, (mud), we can't see, but obedience to the Word given opens the eyes.

Satan, taking opportunity to deceive us, allures us away from the need to see our need for a Savior. He wants to keep us in discouragement by looking at what we don't have instead of what we can have in Jesus Christ.

God does not give us scriptures just to get us to read something. His Word is instruction for us to deal with sins and iniquities within, and has the power to transform our lives into the reality of who we are in Christ. It is God's plan for us to work at rebuilding our lives, but unless the work is with a clean vessel, the work will not profit us. Turn to Ezekiel 36:

33. This is what the Sovereign Lord says: On the day I cleanse you from all your sins, I will resettle your towns and ruins will be rebuilt.

34. The desolate land will be cultivated instead of lying desolate in the sight of all who pass through it.

35. They will say, 'This land that was laid waste has become like the garden of Eden the cities that were lying in ruins, desolate and destroyed, are now fortified and inhabited.

Trusting in God allows us to wait

It is God's plan to remove the disappointments, hurts, flattery, desire for power, and anxieties form our lives as these are as a shroud of death to us. We are told in Isaiah 25 that He will remove this shroud of death that enfolds people because they trusted in Him. We have to trust in God for changes. Then, when the shroud of death is removed, He will prepare a feast of rich foods and a banquet of aged wine, and we would rejoice and be glad in His salvation. Yes, this is speaking of the last days when death is completely swallowed up and it is prophesying of the time when Jesus tasted death for us; but we can also apply this literally for our time because Jesus has already come to change us from death to life.

How can we pray God's Word if we don't know what Jesus has done for us? When knowledge of Him is in our hearts, we have power to proclaim and receive God's Word. Satan might not be able to stop the Word from coming to us, but if he can place something in our heart (discouragement, fear, doubt, lies, etc.), then he knows the Word will not take root and our faith to pray is destroyed.

Hypocrisy stops intercession

Hypocrisy is speaking the Word without knowing the Word. It is a word being sent from our lower nature which is powerless to change others. A word sent from God has power to change situations. (John 1:19). Will we not wait for the Word?

Verse 16 says, "He who listens to you listens to me; he who rejects you rejects me; but he who rejects me rejects Him who sent me." When we cannot hear the voice of God, we have rejected Jesus in that word.

Jesus put a strong emphasis on seeing and hearing in Luke 10:23, "Blessed are the eyes that see what you see. For I tell you that many prophets and kings wanted to see what you see but did not see it, and to hear what you hear but did not hear it."

Disobedience takes us outside of the Kingdom and keeps us from seeing and hearing. It does not necessarily remove us from salvation, but it keeps us from profiting or living within the benefits and blessings of the kingdom. Habakkuk 2:2-3 says,

2.   Write down the revelation and make it plain on tablets so that a herald may run with it.

3.   For the revelation awaits an appointed time; it speaks of the end and will not prove false. Though it linger, wait for it; it will certainly come and will not delay.

God wants those outside of the kingdom to turn and be healed. If He didn't, He wouldn't have sent His Son, Jesus, to die for us. He wants people to pray, like Paul, to be that intercessor to speak God's Word with power. This will require a sacrifice of obedience to God's will and God's way.

Paul tells us in I Corinthians 14 that the church needs to be strengthened, live together in an orderly manner, and operate in the gifts God has given to each of us. As long as one believer is "outside" and not seeing with the eyes of the Spirit, we, as a body, remain fragmented.

Intercession is passionate prayers

Jesus is passionate in His love for us. It will take His passion in us to be able to pray affectively. Without passion we will lack the faith needed to pray according to His Word. Satan knows this, so he does everything to cause us to become weary in our prayers and faith. Passionate love has to go beyond the soul's emotions and affections to covenant love.

Earlier I stated the prophecy of Chuck Pierce that God was going to heal our emotions. When this is done, then a mighty power will arise to defeat Satan's plans by pulling down the stronghold in our minds. A stronghold is a mindset impregnated with hopelessness that causes us to accept, as unchangeable, situations that we know are contrary to the will of God.1 II Corinthians 10:3-5 says:

3. For though we live in the world, we do not wage war as the world does.
4. The weapons we fight with are not the weapons of the world. On the contrary, they have divine power to demolish strongholds.
5. We demolish arguments and every pretension that sets itself up against the knowledge of God, and we take captive every thought to make it obedient to Christ

What a promise! We have the power to demolish every argument and pretension that is against the knowledge of God. To walk in this power, or to appropriate it, we will have to have the passionate love of God for others.

There have been those who have had such a passion for the Word that they meditate on it continually. When they see something in the Word that concerns them, they pursue it with passion. The word, "pursue" means to follow with the view of overtaking, capturing to strive to gain; seek to attain or accomplish; and to proceed in accordance with. We are to pursue prayer by seeing that prayer is bringing forth the Christ. We need to be persistent and pray with fervent heat. These prayers avail much and give us certain rights—they are heard by our Father!

God promises us an inheritance in Christ Jesus. Everything He is belongs to us legally as our inheritance. Some of the gifts that belong to us have been taken from us. We need them back to rebuild. We need to go to God and ask Him to let us recover all that was taken. Isaiah 11:10-11 continues with the following promises:

10. The Root of Jesse will stand as a banner for the peoples; the nations will rally to him, and his place of rest will be glorious.
11. In that day the Lord will reach out his hand a second time to reclaim the remnant that is left of his people.

At the time for change, there is of necessity a "voice" in which someone is praying

We cannot keep calling forth the things which we see in the natural and expect a change. We have to hear the prophetic voice and speak the prophetic voice that God has given to us.

Intercessors pray for others to change—then wait in faith to see them change. God's Word always requires faith in that which He gives to us. We are not to confess our abilities or our desires as the sole reason to obtain or do something. Our confession to possess has to be in that which God has given to us as an inheritance. Ephesians 6:10-12 states this quite clear:

10. Last of all I want to remind you that your strength must come from the Lord's mighty power within you.
11. Put on all of God's armor so that you will be able to stand safe against all strategies and tricks of Satan.
12. For we are not fighting against people made of flesh and blood, but against persons without bodies—the evil rulers of the unseen world; and against huge numbers of wicked spirits in the spirit world.

If our eyes are on the natural world, then we look to natural strengths and power to solve our problems. But if we begin to see behind the veil, we will see spiritual darkness which needs the sword of God's Spirit spoken.

God takes no pleasure in seeing us live a life apart from Him. His love is so strong towards man that He allowed His Son to take our sins. God then involves Himself in us so that we will change. In Isaiah 29 He says,

22. No longer will Jacob be ashamed; no longer will their faces grow pale,

23. when they see among them their children, the work of my hands, they will keep my name holy; they will acknowledge the holiness of Jacob and will stand in awe of the God of Israel.

24. Those who are wayward in spirit will gain understanding; those who complain will accept instruction.

These scriptures promise hope to us who are waiting on our loved ones to see the Lord. We have His promise that those who are of the seed of Abraham, even though they have wandered and have a wayward spirit, will gain understanding and accept instructions.

Intercession is entreating for others

We cannot pray without our mediator, Jesus Christ, who entreats for us on our behalf. Entreat means: to make intercession, intercessor, lay, light upon, meet together, pray, and reach. When we "reach out for Jesus," we show by action that we want Jesus to make intercession for us; to come upon us, and to pray for us so that we can meet together. Isaiah 59:16-21 says that Jesus' arm is outstretched to work salvation for those who call upon Him. To these, He will place His Spirit and His words in our mouths, and in the mouths of our children and descendants from that time on and forever.

We have this hope as an eternal promise from our Lord to intercede for us and reach us when our hope is in Him to deliver. Matthew 7:7 says, "Ask and it will be given to you; seek and you will find; knock and the door will be opened to you. For everyone who asks receives; he who seeks finds; and to him who knocks, the door will be opened."

We decide much of our future by the way we serve God. We can abort the promises by presumption, anxiety, etc. Failure to ask God for help and failure to ask Him for the Word we need cause us to fail.

God is calling intercessors to seek

God is calling forth seekers of God. Seek means to look for, to hunt for. The word seek implies desire to have something or someone. God desires us and wants us to desire Him from our whole heart. We are to long for Him and to have fellowship with Him. We are bidden to come to Him. We are invited to enter God's throne room.

The Sound of the Prodigal

How, you might ask, can a prodigal make a sound and what kind of intercession, would this be? To understand this type of intercession we need to look as some key words from Luke 15:14. They are: After he *spent everything,* there was *a severe famine.* The word "spent" means to be exhausted, used up, useless, depleted, and to be worn out. Severe means harsh, cruel, brutal, difficult, and ruthless.

The intercessor feels these things within himself. He has come to a place in which he feels completely spent and has no energy to even enjoy anything. He is like a zombie going through the motions of life, exhausted, depleted of any love for someone, something, or for self.

What happens at this time is the intercessor will hear two voices. One will identify with giving up, dying, letting it all go, abandonment, etc. or the voice of God telling him to pray in the spirit to build him up (Jude 20-21). A choice is made, not after the void he is feeling, but after obedience to turn to God and pray.

In Ezekiel 37 God asks the prophet, "What do you see?" Ezekiel saw the dry bones. The intercessor will see the dryness of his life. Then comes another voice, "Can these bones live?" Once we decide to live and give ourselves to this intercession, the breath of life comes forth for the person you are interceding for and for the intercessor. Breath, as it is found in Genesis 2:7, means wind, angry, vital breath, divine inspiration, intellect soul, spirit. (7307) to blow-perceive, make of quick understanding, enjoy, and anticipate, to smell and to touch.

Once intercession comes the breath of God comes upon the person to give him quick understanding and the ability to anticipate something happening that will change his circumstances. This is a type of gaining access to the Father on behalf of another who feels like the prodigal.

Romans 5:2 says that we can gain access into this place by faith through our Lord Jesus Christ to establishes His throne. This is what intercession is all about, establishing something in God's love. Isaiah put it this way in chapter 16:

4. . . . When the oppressor is no more, and destruction has ceased, and he who tramples under foot has vanished from the land,

5. then a throne will be established in steadfast love and on it will sit in faithfulness in the tent of David one who judges and seeks justice and is swift to do righteousness."

Do these words sound familiar? They should. God has given them to us in Micah 6:8. "He has showed you, O man, what is good; and what does the Lord require of you but to do justice, and to love kindness, and to walk humbly with your God?"

To sum up the study of intercession and how it relates to the past, present, and future, I quote from "Reading The Old Testament" by Lawrence Boadt, in his definition of archeology:

> Archaeology literally means "the study of beginnings." It is an organized and systematic science of mankind's past, it was given life in 1871 by the electrifying announcement of George Smith, a young creator at the British Museum, that he had been able to read a Babylonian tablet on which he hand found a flood story like that of Noah, but hundreds, perhaps a thousand, years older! The rush to explore the lands of the Bible was on. Every new object or tablet uncovered led to claims and counter-claims and often even wild new guesses about the background of biblical stories.

This is what the art of intercession does. It uncovers hidden mysteries of the past to those in the present so that future events can be changed. Once we experience intercession, we will be so electrified that we will want to keep digging into God's Word so that we can be used again for His glory. Yes, intercession takes work; but, like digging relics from the past holds great joy for some, so will intercession as they see lives rescued from generational curses.

Compensation is a voice to speak

Intercession is work! It is a call of God and He promises us certain things for our faithfulness in obeying Him. The word "compensation" means:

1. Something given or received as an equivalent for services.
2. To counterbalance; offset; to make up for.
3. To provide for an equivalent.

The work that we are being compensated for is found in Revelation 2:17. "He who has an ear, let him hear what the Spirit says to the churches. To him who overcomes, I will give some of the hidden manna. I will also give him a white stone with a new name written on it, known only to him who receives it."

As we look up the word "stone" in the Greek, we see that it represents a pebble used as a verdict; a vote:—stone, voice. We are then directed to another reference, #5584, which means to verify by contact; to search for—feel after, handle, and touch.

The compensation that we receive, "the white stone for overcoming," is something given to us in the present which has a voice to speak for us to the Father our future for past works. It is something that can be read by others. I Peter 2 tells us that Jesus is the living stone which was laid in Zion, a chosen cornerstone. We also, like living stones (chips off the block, so to speak) are to show forth His work done at Calvary.

We are also given "hidden manna." The hidden manna is a Word from God to sustain us in the place that we are in so that we can endure with patience until the time comes for the manifestation of the compensation. This hidden manna gives us the boldness to speak as though we have already received. We have an example of this in Revelation 1:9-11:

John was in a place, (the isle of Patmos), and he was suffering for the Word's sake. He says that he is a companion with his brothers not only in the suffering, but in the kingdom and patient endurance. In this place he hears a word giving him instructions to encourage the church. He tells them that there will be a recompense (compensation) to those who continue in their faithfulness. He also warned the churches that they would experience judgment if they were not faithful.

Compensation is manifested "after" there is patient endurance for the Word's sake. So, each time that we overcome an assignment we are given a Word to sustain us and to encourage us to speak God's Word which brings compensation. The voice might sound something like this: (taken from Psalm 89)

> *Father, as I look at the situation that I am in, (present) which is devastation, You promised me years back (past) that I have a covenant of steadfast love with You. You swore to me that You would establish my line forever and that my descendants would reign in righteousness. Now, with that Word from You, I look to my future and see the fulfillment of that Word. As it is written in I Peter, I am a living stone with Your Word written on my forehead. Your Word will speak as a voice for me and for my future generations. I groan in the spirit until that Word is visualized.*

David was compensated for having a heart after God with a covenant of promise for his descendants. When things came to take his heart from God, he overcame the temptation and remained steadfast in his love. As compensation for this, David was given a covenant that would speak for him far into the future even when David was dead. This "voice" which spoke for David was picked up by intercessors even today for all those who are of that seed.

Prophecy

Breaker

Believe in Me and the best is yet to come—even now. Know that it is upon you says the Lord. It is in My rest that you will find the end of self and the beginning of Me.

Do not be weary in this season. Run the race. It is in running the race that you will see My face. Do not be weary, you are in training—building muscles to run the race. Do not give up—but press toward Me. There is a miracle that is at your reach. Believe in Me.

In Me is everything you need to feed—to nurture. Healing is here to open eyes in this season to those who cannot see or hear. Multitudes will come to you so that they can see and hear because of Me.

Break through to break out!

Given by Rev. Mary Renteria
2005

Reference

The Book
Tyndale House Publishers, Inc.
Wheaton, Illinois Pg. 886

Possessing your Inheritance by Chuck D. Pierce & Rebecca Wagner Sytsema
Regal Books from Gospel Light
Ventura, California, U.S.A.

[1.] Possessing your Inheritance by Chuck D. Pierce & Rebecca Wagner
Sytsema—Regal Books from Gospel Light
Ventura, California, U.S.A. page 124

Books of Destiny
Streams Publishing House
P.O. Box 550, North Sutton, New Hampshire 03260

[2.] Illustrated Davis Dictionary of the Bible
The Old-Time Gospel Hour Edition
C-1973 Royal Publishers, Inc.
P.O. Box 47 * Nashville, TN 37202
Pg. 567

American College Dictionary
School Library Addition
Random House, New York

Illustrated Davis Dictionary of the Bible
The Old-Time Gospel Hour Edition
Copyright 1973 Royal Publishers, Inc.
P.O. Box 47 Nashville, TN 37202

Attila the Hun:
Http://WWW.ralm-of-shade.comzarathustr/Atilla.html

Hannibal: Hannibal Barca: Military Genius by Adel Beshara
Http://WWW.ssnp.comhanibal.htm

Quest Study Bible
New Internal Version

Thorndike-Barnhard Comprehensive Desk Dictionary.

New Standard Bible, Foundation press

Open Bible, Thomas Nelson, Publishers
Nashville. Camden. New York

Strong's Exhaustive Concordance
James K. Strong
Baker Book House
Grand Rapids, Michigan

Wycliffe Bible Commentary
Moody Press
Chicago, Ill.

Matthew Henry's Commentary
Matthew Henry
Zondervan Publishing House
Grand Rapids, Michigan

Expository Dictionary of Bible Words
Lawrence O. Richards
Zondervan Publishing House
Grand Rapids, Michigan

Benny Hinn Media Ministries
Orlando, Florida

Jewish New Testament
David H. Stern
The Messianic Jewish Movement International
Bethesda, MD. 20824 (USA)

The Blood Covenant
H.Clay Trumbull
Impact Books, Inc.
Kirkwood, Mo.

Exploring Worship
Judson Cornwall

New American Standard Bible
Foundation Press
Anaheim, Calif.

The Spiritual Warfare by Dr. Ed Murphy
Thomas Nelson Publishers
Nashville-Atlanta-London-Vancouver
Page 508, The Road to Personal Victory in Spiritual Warfare

Reading The Old Testament by Lawrence Boadt
Paulist Press
New York, N.Y. Mahwah, N.J.
Pages 52-53

The Holy Bible
Revised Standard Version
Thomas Nelson & Sons
New York